"It will cost you."

Thirty Dollars and a Bowl of Soup

by Carla M. Cherry

———— THE SECOND EDITION ————

iiPUBLISHING

Thirty Dollars and a Bowl of Soup
Copyright © 2021 by Carla M. Cherry

Second Edition

Copyright notice
All rights reserved. No part of this book may be reproduced in any form or by any electronic or mechanical means, including information storage and retrieval systems, without permission in writing from the author or publisher, except for the use of brief quotations in a book review.

Cover design by tonii

ISBN: 978-1-7362167-7-4

Printed in the United States of America

iiPUBLISHING
New York, NY
www.toniiinc.com

Note

Thirty Dollars and a Bowl of Soup was my second book of poetry, and it was comprised of poems written from 2009-2017. I self-published the first edition of *Thirty Dollars and a Bowl of Soup* through Wasteland Press in 2017. I am extremely grateful to the beautiful work that Tim Veeley, president of Wasteland Press, did on the formatting and designing cover art for first edition, and I will always be proud of it.

Thanks to iiPublishing, I have been able to transition from self-publishing to traditional publication. I am grateful for their work on this second edition

This edition includes several new poems: "Bonanza", "Redress", and "For the Record.".

Acknowledgements

First and foremost, I would like to express my love for my mother, my son Khari, my niece Anike, and my cousin Eric for inspiring the title of this book. I would like to thank my best friend Tanya for reading and critiquing many of the poems in this book, my sister Donna for her help with formatting the manuscript, my friend Richard, his lovely wife Hatshepsut, and Tony Flags for providing the music for my recordings of some of the poems in this book. I'm also grateful to Oka Obono who encourages my writing from across the Atlantic Ocean. Finally, Soraya, Caroline, Wiatta, Nikki, Maria, Tahirah, Terrence, and Carlton, I am eternally grateful for your friendship.

Jazz. The only
true American music
We study the
Masters. Practice, compose
and oh the
way we improvise,
and sometimes all
they give you
is ***thirty dollars
and a bowl
of soup.***

CONTENTS

I Chrysocolla

Philosophy of the Line	1
Going Beyond	2
Green	5
Juice	6
The Bronx	8
First Time	10
Bonanza	12
Hands	15
Pupil	16
Swinging	18
Good Kentucky Stock	20
The Second Deadly Sin	22

II Abalone

The Following	27
Cold Blooded	28
Give Me Some Sugar	29
A Poem of Thanksgiving	30
If I Were a Book	32
Common	34
Secrets in the Modern Age	36
Against the Grain	38
First and Last	41
Grandmother's Wisdom	42
Confession	45
Damage	46
Tamale	48
Morning at the Museum	50

Aventurine III

54	How Do You Say It?
56	Out of the Ordinary
59	Run for Cover
61	If He Knows a Mango
62	Marks
64	We Were Cooking Sunday Dinner
66	Honeymoon in Cerulean
68	Hard Candy

Goldstone IV

73	Freed Up
75	You Can Find True Love in a Butterfly Cinquain
77	Haiku for Khari
78	Aftermath of the Great American Celebration
80	Yankee Girl Reverie
82	The Unwelcome
85	Emergence
86	I Shouldn't Have Been There
88	Boycott
89	For Jordan Russell Davis
90	A Rondine of the Rhetorical Kind
91	When a Plus Is Not
92	I'll Be Damned
94	Privilege
97	Hold
98	Diaspora

No Access	100
To Work	102
Machines	104
Witness	106
Disclosure	108

V Jasper

Dear Yoko Ono	115
For Osmel Sousa	116
Teal	117
In the Moment	118
For Bree Newsome	119
Perceptions	120
For Sista Gaines	126
Movement	130
On the Mend	132
Ode to Pannetta and Wannett	134
Absolution	138
Accountable Talk	143
Trigger Alert	144
Stroking	146
Connections	150
Resistance	152
Redress	154
How Far We've Come	157

158	Child's Play
160	She Hid It Well
163	Sisterhood
165	This Is Why I Smile at My Friend Soraya
166	Love Letter
169	Thank You, Amber Rose
171	Kanye West
173	Objectified

Jade VI

176	Perigee Moon
178	Will Love Trump Hate
183	What Matters
184	For the Record
189	Fixed
191	On Your Departure

I | Chrysocolla

Philosophy of the Line

The straight line intimidates--tall buildings. Poetry.
We are hard-wired with a predilection for curves.
It is why I hate walking around bedrooms, living rooms.

Lost count of the small purple bruises accrued on a thigh, a calf
from squeezing curves past sharp corners jutting out
from bed frames, coffee tables, nightstands.

The poetic line. Mull every word, comma, dash, period.
Sing along to Jill Scott,
bop and bump to Erykah Badu.
Still, my poems--this poem--mostly resemble
rectilinear skyscrapers with short lines, hanging terraces for long ones.

Highlines. Can't stand on balconies for long--
knees buckle a little. Imagine a free fall,
thwack of bone and flesh on concrete.

Curves. Why my baby, her baby, any baby
quieted quicker on my sister's bosom than mine.
Why I like my cursive better than my print.

It is why, when I read bras
constrict flow of collagen, lymph, nutrients--
I happily set them aside for work only.

Learning to love my own bounce and quiver.
Going to keep playing with poetic words, lines
until it feels natural to let them sway across the page.

Going Beyond

When I discovered I could not tuck moonlight into my pocket
and add it to my family of things I picked up a pen instead.

This stripping my soul naked ain't always easy
for me, a woman who doesn't like tight dresses.

Poems come to me   in dreams   every now and then I

stumble in the dark to my desk turn on the light
scribble furiously in black ink.

Bruise my leg on my bed frame sometimes
when poems come to me in dreams
and I stumble in the dark to my desk.

Ask myself why I bother every now and then
with this stripping my soul naked and sharing.

My poems get compliments and some get published.
I have some bruises but sometimes my poems

turn on

a light.

Green

Mrs. Lewis gave each of us
a rexographed picture
of a flower.

I inhaled the ink.
It tickled my nose.

I scribbled methodically.
Stayed within the black lines.

When she passed by my masterpiece,
she yelled at me--
I had colored
stem
leaves
petals
my favorite green.

Neck, hot comb hot.
Vision blurred
by tears and shame,
I ground my purple crayon into the paper
bleeding the petals into midnight blue.

I was one of the best readers
in her kindergarten class.

And if she'd had a heart,
I would have explained my vision--
I'd only wanted to replicate
the verdant beauty of spring.

Juice

Slick, pink frosted lipstick, pink pantsuits.
Six feet tall, silver-streaked black hair piled on top of her head
made her even taller. Gravelly, smoky voice. Never smiled.
Even the air in the classroom was still.
Displease her, get a hard tug on your ear.
I was quiet, diligent. Spent my entire first grade year in fear.
Had a metal lunch box with the characters from The Rescuers on it.
Every day Mommy packed it with liverwurst, bologna, or ham sandwiches,
a Hostess chocolate cupcake, and a canned Mott's juice.
On the walk to school each day, gently swung my lunchbox along,
letting it bounce out a metal tune against my leg,
anticipating wistful glances at my cupcake from Sejal,
my pretty classmate whose mother always sent her green grapes as dessert.
One day Mommy packed my favorite flavor of juice, fruit punch.
Only drank half at lunch. Wanted to save it for later.
Stuck it inside my lunch box,
placed it back in my cubby. At the end of the day, pulled out my lunchbox--
huge droplets of pink juice dripped onto the floor.
Oh no.

I had looked forward to the dulcet end to my school day,
letting the last few gulps course down my throat before my afternoon snack.
Knowing I had caused what would become a sticky mess,
I approached my teacher, pointed towards the offending spot on the floor.
Mrs. Berman, I spilled my juice.
 She immediately pushed me to the floor, tossed me a sponge,
growled at me to clean it up.
"Now I'm going to be late getting home to my poor sick husband!"
Tears welled in my eyes, my ears and neck hot like embers.
She loomed over me in her pink pantsuit frowning,
right hand jabbed into her right hip.
I mopped up my pink nightmare,
silently whipping myself for not sidestepping the spill,
letting the custodian clean it up.
My classmates put on their coats and book bags in silence,
afraid sympathetic looks, offers to help,
would earn them a tongue lashing or an ear pulling.
When the school year came to its merciful end, she hugged all of us goodbye.
When it was my turn,
I stood still long enough for her to put her arms around me and ran.

The Bronx

Was in a workshop, teacher asked where we're from
Two of us said The Bronx is from where we come.
His joke--we could guard each other on the way home.
Wanted to pick up a book and lob it at his dome.

Opened notebook instead to talk about the chirping birds,
early morning and evening.
Blue jays, red-breasted robins. Swallows.
Raccoons. Rabbits. Groundhogs. Watch your step--
more goose droppings than shootings, though.

Hip hop. Parents hated it.
O'Jays, Blue Magic, Harold Melvin
and the Blue Notes were more their style.
Patti LaBelle and the Blue Bells. Singing Lady Marmalade in the courtyard,
swinging our little clueless hips to the naughtiness sliding from our lips.
The sound of clackers could be heard for half a mile.
Don't hit your hands with 'em.
Red light green light 1 2 3. Gotta turn around before you run up on me.

Handball courts. Aimed for that blue ball, always missed.
Open fire hydrant for sweet water sips.

Boom boxes. Break dancing. My poses followed by falls.
Right On! magazine. Michael Jackson, Prince, Five Star on my walls.
Candy rings. Bubble gum cigarettes. Razzamatazz. I chewed all day long.
Fun Dip, Lik-a-Stik. Sugar candy poured in my hand. Blow Pops.
If you don't lick it hard three times you won't reach the soft chewy center.

Hopscotch. Firecrackers and foot stomping poppers on the 4th of July.
Big Wheels, rolling down the hill.

Come see my puppy.
Never that 'cause we don't know you.
Where is Etan Patz?

Leaned blossoming backside against boyfriend.
Somebody's mama told me it's wrong.
In those days, we listened.
Struggling/working/middle class
we had style all the while.
 Lee jeans, all colors, from Fordham Road.
Gold name chains. Initialed and two-finger rings.
Leather and lumberjack jackets.

Cars roll by blasting rap/R&B/bachata/salsa--
I shout, that's my song!
I shimmy my shoulders, sing along.

Don't need an armed guard.
Got wit like a dagger, plenty of swagger.

First Time

It is new--
brick red
white vinyl tassels
a bell
for a happy fifth birthday.

Training wheels laid to the side.
Hold me, Daddy!
Don't let go!

Assured of his grip on the back of the seat
legs pump unsteadily
arms slowly straightening up
and out
then the
cutting through air.

With that sudden light feeling
turned around to see
where Daddy went,
waved at his retreating figure.

Bike wobbled and turned over.
Blood and white meat on knee.

He dusted her off softly
until the sniffling stopped.

He wondered if they should stop,
go home,
sing the birthday song,
and cut the cake,

but they are black
she is a girl
she is his eldest

and he's been throwing her up in the air
since she was a baby
so she'll fall in love with aiming high.

He said,
Get back on.
Time to ride.

Bonanza

First son of a first son of a first son,
Daddy's first child was supposed to be
a boy named Russell
who would mimic his walk and laughter,
watch, then help him fix cars,
soak up his wisdom about the world and women.
Surrounded by three sets of round hips with
determined mouths,
he was the head of household.
The hardest thing in our house,
sometimes his stern bass bounced off the walls but
he was hugs and handholding.
We had a set of encyclopedias
books
toy trucks
dolls and dollhouses
piano, flute, dance lessons
computer classes

rug hooking sets
science kits
plastic looms to make potholders
and my sister passed him the wrenches he needed.
When I learned what my name would have been
I asked if he was sorry about being the only man in the house.
He said daughters showed more love than sons.
Even as twentysomethings
we ran to the top of the stairs
to watch him walk up,
bounced in place
calling daddy, daddy.
He did not even try to hide his smile
as we stretched out our arms.
Saying I love you
or telling us we were beautiful was not his way
but his showing over telling
made him the best kind of poet.

Hands

Last night after washing the last of the dinner dishes,
sweeping the kitchen floor, and carrying the garbage out,
I lit lavender incense and collapsed on my sofa.

Looked down at my hands. Cuticles, dry and thick
from constant hand washing with harsh school soap/
writing on chalkboards/washing them clean.

Went to my bedroom for the cocoa butter on my dresser.
As I moistened and massaged my hands, I studied
the slight upward bend of my fingertips. They are like my father's.

Flecks of black grease dotted our sink
after Daddy washed his hands of long days
handling baggage at the airport and fixing our neighbors' cars.

Donna and I teased him about his ashy hands. He laughed
and began keeping a tiny white tube of Curacel in his car.
I'd watch him shake the lotion down into his palms
rubbing his long brown fingers until they had a light fragrant sheen.

The day Daddy spoke his final morphine-induced words--
Your mother was here
Donna and I stroked his hands.
We clipped his fingernails, each time more gently than the last
when he flinched.

After the funeral home
placed one hand on top of the other
we admired their manicured look.

Pupil

Bookish me should have been by Daddy's side
while he was under the hoods of his Volvos
or the cars of our neighbors;

with shiny silver tools in hand
he kept us safe, for cheap.

Should have asked him to name the parts
all those wires and hoses were connected to
as he twisted this, tugged that.

Ten years, 7 months, 2 days since I could ask him
how to check the oil and the tire pressure
or how to find the carburetor.

Because he would never again call one of us to bring one of his wrenches
or suck his teeth and go get it himself,
we gave his brick red and black multi-shelf tool cabinet to our cousin--
one less thing around to make us cry.

Mommy, at 77,
is up and down the stairs with ease,
quick to laugh at her favorite films,
headphones on ears, framed photos of Johnny Mathis on her bedroom walls.

She used to take us to Lamston's in the Bartow mall,
us girls tugging her arms, as she
browsed the aisles for just the right brightly colored yarn.

I used to watch her sit on the sofa,

TV on, right leg tucked under left
her clicking needles deftly weaving perfectly symmetrical,
diagonal rows of warmth
hardly looking down at her hands, just like when she typed.

Me, the eldest, never crafted much--
little potholders or small rugs. Easy.
The loom came with directions; the rug hooking sets
came with color-coded mesh and matching yarn.

Had one sewing class in sixth grade, only
finished one of three projects--a crooked apron made from
discarded brown and blue cloth found in Mommy's sewing chair.

I know one day my sister and I
will sit in Mommy's bedroom
beside the pile of knitted afghans
and decide whom will get which.

I know the two I want for sure--the
rose and mauve,
cream and periwinkle.

The forest and kelly green one still has the sagging gap
from years of us snuggling underneath,
kicking each other and giggling.

Proud me, who doesn't like to fail,
should let Mommy teach me and
stop pretending she will always be around
to sew up that stupid hole

Swinging

Took me a little while to learn how.
Didn't need Mommy or Daddy to push me from behind once I was
putting my feet hard to the ground, pulling backward on the metal chains
lifting my legs/turning my thighs in and out/pulling my calves backward for
momentum.

Nothing like flying through the air/making my own breeze/
ignoring gum popping girls who rolled their eyes/sucked teeth/yelled
"Hurry up!"

Sometimes I wish I had been one of those kids who knew
how to jump off, land perfectly on the blacktop.

Liked unbroken bones too well.
Always stopped by dragging my feet.

Had I risked scrapes or busted arms,
maybe I would be one of those women who
zip lines in the rain forest
hikes up mountaintops
jumps off low cliffs to swim
or makes love under waterfalls in broad daylight.

Then again, I am a big city girl.
Hospitals abound.
What's to stop me from
going in a park
once all the kids are gone
sliding these motherly hips through metal chains
pumping legs
swinging high
jumping off
aiming for a perfect landing on the blacktop

Good Kentucky Stock

Favorite family photograph:
Great-grandmother Florence, in the lower left-hand corner
surrounded by her sisters: Emma, Molly, Margaret, and Nannie.
Hangs on my living room wall, to the right of Grandma Pauline's portrait.
Florence was the darkest, and, I think, the most beautiful--
but not for her deep brown unmarked skin, large dark eyes;
it's the unflinching gaze.
She died the year before my mother was born.
Mommy has her eyes and jawline.
I have her bow-shaped lips.

I asked her youngest daughter, my aunt LaVerne
(her middle name, we can't use her first)
to tell me what she remembers about her:

There had been a drought.
Aunt Verne was sitting on the porch while Florence cooked potatoes
Great-grandpa James threatened to split her head open
with a two by four if she opened her mouth.
Florence sat next to Aunt Verne and soothed her as she cried.
Next day she went to town for a divorce.
Remarried later--gentle William, and Aunt Verne loved to sit on his lap until
Florence told her she was too big for that.

Florence, as Grandma Pauline once said, was good:
Used cord to fashion her three daughters' hair into silky curls
drew water from the well
chopped snakes with a hoe
killed chickens from the coop by hand
cured and hung hams
grew apples in their orchard for pies, made jellies,
fresh ice cream for summer, with snow on top in the winter
baked angel food cake in the coal burning stove
picked grapes from the arbor for communion wine
made communion crackers for Goodloe's Chapel Baptist,
and she would have loved my sister and me.
When people tell me I am strong or smart, I smile and sometimes
wish I could have come along for her bad-ass, dusty march into town.

The Second Deadly Sin

I love plants. Mommy always grew them. Ferns. Dieffenbachia.
Philodendron.
Because their furry leaves tickled my fingers, my favorite were her African
violets.

In first grade, we were given kidney beans to plant.
Yes! My turn!

When I got home, Mommy gave me a small apricot-colored pot.
Scooped out cupfuls of soil.

I buried my bean. Watched. Waited. When the sprouts emerged,
saturated them with water. Again and again and again.

A month later every kidney-shaped table
in the classroom was embellished by blooming plants, except by my seat.

Hard-headed, still. My friends laugh at the way
I slurp my drinks. You go in, they say.

Yesterday, saw a cinnamon bun boasting a layer of vanilla cream.
Bought two--ten-dollar minimum for a credit card purchase.

Licked, sucked the icing from the last bite of the first and second
from my fingers and lips. Felt nauseous.

Why is it we can only have a little sweetness?
Must train myself to sip/savor, sip/savor,

not consume a pint of coconut ice cream in one sitting,
even though I am happiest when I can spoon,

when it is between my lips, tongue pressing vanilla/mocha sweetness tightly
against the roof of my mouth, then melting, then flowing leisurely down my
throat.

Only one cupful a day until the occasional pint is empty.
I cannot squeeze much of its aftermath into my shrinking jeans.

II | Abalone

The Following

In those days we snickered as we drew flawless hearts
Over lowercase I's and J's.
Do you like me or Keisha? Would you go out with Tito? Check yes or no.
Take a survey--who is the cutest or funniest or best-dressed?
Folded them into perfect squares.
Passed them under our desks, behind teachers' turned backs.

When I saw Sean I stopped the giggling. He was in the tenth grade,
I was in the ninth. Cashew-colored skin, cocoa brown eyes,
hair so wavy I know
he wore a du-rag each night.
He must have shopped on Fordham Road.
Had the latest style Lee jeans, I-zod shirts,
and sheepskin coat for the winter.

We were in Sequential Math I with Mrs. Sprung;
sarcastic woman never smiled.
He sat by the window, in the front.
I sat on the opposite side, by the wall, glad he could not see me staring
from behind thick glasses, underneath shapeless wool coat.

I once followed behind him all the way
down to the basement
just so I could inhale his cologne.

He never turned around, never spoke.
I had to walk back up four flights
to get to Spanish class.
I was late,
out of breath,
damp with sweat,
crushed.

Cold Blooded:
Why I Hung Up Last Night and Blocked Your Number

Had I known the connection between the iris and the frontal lobe,
I would have:
invited you on a midnight walk,
pointed at the North Star,
asked you to focus,
sat you down on a rock,
tilted your head back,
stood over you with a flashlight,
studied your pupils.

I suspect
I would have found more contraction furrows
than crypts
in thy frugal eyeballs.

Give Me Some Sugar

There's nothing going on but sleep between my sheets.
And it's because I crave me a special something sweet.

Not Godiva. Not chocolate chips.
But soothing words from your lips:

"I'll cook tonight." "I'm proud of you,".
Best of all, "I love you too."

Don't know where you are where you're from
how you'll look, or when You'll come.

But when God puts you in my path
You'll protect me and make me laugh.

Thank me for each meal I'll cook
With a smile and Come hither look.

And even when we scream and shout
We'll hunker down and work it out.

Some may say I'm picky with men out there to meet.
But I will wait upon The One, my special something sweet.

A Poem of Thanksgiving

This poem wants to thank all the fathers and mothers
who teach their sons to
open car and building doors,
bring flowers on dates,
and walk on the side of the curb
for us ladies;

and put up a big middle finger
to those of you who raise males like this one:

"Excuse me!"
He fell in step beside me.

"You have to give me your number."

My peripheral vision revealed--
a baseball cap on top of hair slightly streaked with gray,
high top sneakers: the type to hang out on the corner.

"I like your hair. Your dress. You look good."

He was still astride me. Since politeness helps:
"Thank you. I am in a rush."

"Wait, slow down. You jiggling, baby.
You're messing it up."

Could feel his eyes snaking down my body
as I strode a little faster.

"I'm sorry, but I have to go."

"You have to give me your number.
What is your name?"

Running through New York City traffic
would have been suicidal.
I stared at the light, willing it red.

"I'm gonna call you yum-yum
because you are delicious!"

I tried to stop myself but I burst out laughing
as I ran down the stairs into the subway.

When the train came, I sat down and noticed
a gentleman in a suit, his dark skin smoothly polished as
as his shoes.

Right leg over the left,
reading a newspaper.

I smiled.
He never looked up.

If I Were a Book

If I were a book
would you caress my spine?

Would you hold me close to inhale my scent?
Would you mull over the table of contents
then hold each page
between your fingertips?

Would you read me cover to cover,
word for word?

If I were a book
would you write notes in the margins
highlight your favorite phrases?

Would you fold down
your favorite pages?

If I were to be obtuse
would you take the time
to read between the lines,
or would you skip around chapters
and peek at the end?

Would you write your name on the first page?
Would it be in pencil, or permanent ink?

I am not a first, but a limited edition.
Would you take me out of circulation?

Would you call a friend to rave about me,
If I were a book?

Common

I was lounging at Red Rooster with Yolanda and Dee
and the two men Dee met at Corner Social, Michael and Baraka, came over.

Then i was pushed off into a corner,
unsure if it was the glasses i wear because
i was looking hot in red sandals/white top/black wrap/jeans rolled up to
show off shapely calves.
Baraka the tall handsome one, 39, single, with two baby mamas he didn't
marry because they wouldn't cook. Now that he was drinking/disheveled,
and into Dee anyway, thought:
it is just as well.

Just sipped the fruit punch that Michael the married one bought to keep me
occupied, while he flirted with Yo and explained why he took off his ring
when he went out without his wife.

i was taking in the ambience and they started talking about how hard it is
to be single
and Yo says i needed to join the conversation.

Michael said
there are a lot of diseases out here like herpes and HIV
and being single is scary
and Dee says
yeah but being married can be even scarier because of the men who cheat
and Baraka says
        you have to pay a lot for clean pussy
I said, what did he say?
Yolanda repeated it.

I said, what do you mean by clean pussy?

he said there are some chicks and I cut him off
why does she have to be a chick a chick is a baby chicken
and what do you call a man who sleeps with a chick
and Baraka said what do you call him
and I said I'm asking you

Baraka said well chick is a colloquialism, and
I said I know what a colloquialism is
and it doesn't justify your double standard.
Why do you feel comfortable disrespecting us?

With the joy sucked out of my evening I told them I was going outside.
Yolanda asked where and I said I don't know, I just need some air.

Baraka apologized (to impress Yolanda)
but Daddy raised me better than to waste wisdom on a dude
who may not have had a father to teach him—
discerning women who cook willingly are earned with love, commitment,
and honorable purpose.

It ain't easy holding out for the right thing
but it's better than partnered misery.
I stood in the glare of the bright lights outside the throngs of couples and
singles on the prowl thinking I might go home alone
but Yolanda and Dee came out.

Dee said, see, that's why I let my friends introduce me to men.

Off we went, our hips swaying in unison to the beat of our heels
click-clacking against Harlem pavement.

Secrets in the Modern Age

His voice--honey drips and soft licks.
The handsome that evaded me in high school. College.
Hours of exchange--jobs, kids, past relationships. Laughter. Flirtation.
High hopes when he recited lines of my poetry back to me.
Intrigued by my celibacy. Said he thinks I'm ready. He wanted to meet.
Drinks with casual me in sleek dress/heels.
I want/need passion. Love. Trust. Commitment.
He wants revealing pics, yet

This temple is for one who worships.

He liked the pic of me in my royal purple dress--
I have "a fat ass". Dug my ceiling high bookshelves.
Liked my voice too, its husky softness, and
my gift of gab--" you could talk your way out of a murder rap".
He wanted to see my bare derriere. I sent one of its contours.
In return, I got a text. "Why didn't you take off the panties?"
It's my time, I said. *You know.*
I heard my father's voice. "He's not strong enough for you."
Three years of longing/withholding yet

This temple is for one who worships.

He asked to see my vaginal lips. Dozens of shots, every angle--
Wait. Models don't do shots that close.
D'Angelo didn't sing how does it look, but "how does it feel"?
Sent a pic featuring my textbook-perfect toothy smile.
He said I lie too much. His pics/texts/number all erased.
I want/need passion. Love. Trust. Commitment.
Daddy smiling down on me.

This temple is for one who worships.

Against the Grain

What are you hiding, he asked her when
she first said she doesn't shave.

That is some 1970s shit, he said.
You got an Angela Davis afro down there?

She looked up salons
that would do the do

but recoiled at
hot wax
sharp objects
near
strong
safe
sensitive
space.

She remembered
the one thing her last got right--
his refusal to wash her away before he left,
inhaling her all the way home.

God grew her bushy curtain, age 5.
Her mother instructed--
cleanse gently
mild soap and water, daily.

She'd sit in the bathtub, quietly curling
dewy hair around soapy fingers.

At camp she sneaked behind other girls undressing,
wondering after their baldness, always
proud to be ahead.

As a woman
beautiful, naturally lush
sister doctors instructed--
cleanse gently,
mild soap and water, daily.

She laughed to herself
at his promise,
if she be hairless--
to nestle tongue
in her strong
sensitive
shield against infections
and
suck
lick
exhale her
to ecstatic, thigh quaking/shivering

as if
"I want to fuck you"
was enough to tame herself
into prepubescent waxen uniformity
or a landing strip like an airport.

First and Last

Didn't ask anything about me
all evening except
if you could rub my feet

The chirapsia over my bunions, too,
had me all moonflower
til you asked when you could
ease fingers and tongue
into my honeypot

Still hadn't asked me
anything about myself, then
I was all morning glory

Damn, brother
Since you want to
to give me head while
you ignore
what's in mine

gotta keep
these size 16 hips to myself.

When Mr. Right comes for
sapiosexual me

his dick will get
a hug like no other

Grandmother's Wisdom
(for Sallie Cherry)

I.
As a little girl, I once spent the night
at Nana and Pop Pop's house. When she put me to bed
Nana told me to take off my panties.
I always kept them on at home but I did what she said.
Felt naked. Raw. Wrong.

II.
Didn't think about Nana's admonition again. Until him,
who asked me to take a picture of my vagina and text it.
Stripped.
Felt naked. Raw. Wrong.
Took several, from different angles--
my plump ebony lips/clitoris
unlike airbrushed photos and textbook illustrations.
Daubed myself with pejoratives.
Hit delete.
Put my panties back on.
Let him sulk. Speculate. Seek the willing.

III.
Began to wonder about my normalcy. Read.
Discovery--for optimal vaginal health
the first thing a woman should do upon arriving home
is to whip off her panties.

IV.
My daily ritual now--
Whip them off.
Cover up when proper company comes.

Before slumber, shower.
Dry off/bedew.
Hit the lights/lay upon sheets.
Open blinds/windows/legs wide
Bathe/bask in moonlight.

Confession

"Some people say that chocolate
substitutes for sex," he said
as he passed by my table.

I laughed, tongue lightly siphoning
gooey chocolate and whipped cream from my teeth.

A friend said,
"You make it sound like she's not getting any."

"Yeah," I replied.
"You're making a lot of assumptions, brother."

When he asked me to dance
I let him press chiseled chest
tightly against mine.

Inhaled beer and brawn
from his neck.

Didn't move his hands when
they slipped too low
below my waist.

Damage

This morning Pastor said Satan
reminds us of our pasts to distract us
from divine destiny.

It must be why, as I am soulmate seeking,
the same kind of man keeps showing up--
with eyes and hands anxious to undress
after I asked God to send me the right kind.

I get hurt when I rush through the waiting,
just like my car crash:

>   Both of us at stop signs, his van
>   arriving a shade before--
>   me, facing straight ahead
>   he about to turn left.
>
>   I waited for a few moments as he
>   stopped to look for traffic.
>
>   I thought, hey, I have the right of way.
>   He's turning.
>   I am late. I can make it.
>
>   People do it all the time.
>
>   I forge ahead
>   and so does he.
>
>   Before I can stop
>   there is the crunch of metal
>   and my front fender grazing the ground.

We both get out. Argue.
He says his daughter's knee hurts.

After I am calm, I walk up to his car. Apologize.
His little girl was sitting in the rear
with widened eyes of blue,
like her father's.

Although she was unhurt
I sobbed inconsolably
even after he told me not to cry.

Lord.
Help me to slow my speed
my steps
my lustful heart.

If I am tempted
to rush
may I remember
widened eyes of blue
and my front fender grazing the ground

Tamale

Go on and have her. She--
every strand straightened/flowing/swinging left to right in blowing wind.

Flawless face--
plucked eyebrows in perfect arches/licks of mascara
elongating lashes, real and false
glossy lips in shades of merlot/bubble gum pink/electric purple

fingernails buffed to perfect ovals
painted weekly in shades
of merlot/bubble gum pink/electric purple

jeans/dresses tethered, outlining curves of bosom/hips/thighs
slim heels hitting concrete as
the warriors/hunters/traveling men jerk their heads.
Take long pauses, contemplating copulating.

She's a hot tamale.

Me?

I am meant for the settled type--
up at sunrise, off to the same place, same time
every effort made to be home by sundown
kisses on the back of my neck
honey I'm homes
my turn to cook/do the dishes tonight whispered in ear
sittings on sofa reading/movies/ writing out the bills;
I'm sorries when we fight. Luscious lovings that make my
cherry-red painted toes curl
and enfolding me in his arms
for every sunrise.

In ancient and modern times tamales fed
warriors/hunters/travelers.
I ain't lying--I looked it up.
I get it.
She's a hot tamale. I'm a slow burn.
My time/turn for love will come.

Morning at the Museum

This Buddha statue has hollow spaces
where the hands should be.

The other limbs are intact--
are we meant to hold on to nothing?

Desire leads to suffering.
Perhaps love is nothing I should want.

If I follow The Eightfold Path--Right View
Resolve
Speech
Action
Livelihood
Effort
Mindfulness
Concentration

will my soul know solace
whether love finds me

or I succumb, solo,
in a grove of sala trees

Part III | Aventurine

How Do You Say It?

Algo mas?
she said, smiling.

"I'm sorry, what?"

I said, "She means, do you want anything else?"
"Oh," he said. "No, thank you."
"See, 'mas" means "more" and "algo" means something."

I sat, ready to snatch the nouns and the verbs.

He tells her, in Spanish, that he is learning to speak the language and that he is going to start reading *La Prensa, El Diario,* and *El Mundo.*

She tells him, in Spanish, that she doesn't speak English.

I said, "Gracias." when she passed him the bill.
She said, "De nada."

I said,"That means you're welcome."
He said, "That I know."

I said, "I understood everything she said to you and everything you said to her. I just can't speak it."

The last time I tried to converse in a Spanish restaurant I said "tetas" after two minutes of asking the waitress for rice and chicken breasts. Pero, I got my meal.

It was almost two a.m. in Spanish Harlem. We each had a small plate of frijoles negros y arroz and talked about being in our early forties. My son. The clowns I dated on the internet. Real estate. How he knew the Jungle Brothers and A Tribe Called Quest in high school.

It took us a little while to find that friendly little Mexican joint with the sabroso black beans and rice. I just wish they had some platanos, tambien. But hey, it was almost 2 a.m. in Spanish Harlem.

The first spot he had found had a little raton running around by the door, and the next three were about to close.

We had been driving around because he said we should break bread. He ate before the movie, we both had three small bags of popcorn during the flick, and I had said I wasn't hungry. I don't like to eat after eight.

"Come on," he had said. "You can have a little something. Rice and beans." He just wanted us to keep talking, because after three years, I finally said yes.

Out of the Ordinary

Eating a cookie always leaves a mess.
Each time I eat one
I have to hold
my shirt by its bottom
so I don't drop crumbs on the floor--
just in the trash.

Why does Steve Harvey
call the vagina--
feminine sex--
the cookie?

Whether crispy or moist, it is a
scrumptious
singular
object
gone most often
in an instant.

But when we are ready, to love,
I will spread my legs
slide my hands underneath my hips
and raise them to your lips

All you would need
or want to do
after you finish eating is
come up
and kiss me
Let me see if I really do
taste
like orange Now & Laters.

Over the years we can raid the kitchen,
experiment with different flavors--
Strawberry. Pineapple. Peach. Kiwi. Mango

Run for Cover

To say we all need love and affection
is a blanket statement

but it is why I waited so long.
Now that you've said those three words

Come lay next to me.
Keep me warm like a baby wrapped
in its blanket.

So glad you're here.

The last one
left me cold
like a blanket of snow

If He Knows a Mango

A mango.
I knew he was the one when I watched him
eat a mango. Offered him a knife,
he waved me away. *No thanks. What's the rush?*
Ambled to the sink, flicked on faucet,
held mango under water, shook off the excess,
smiled. *Watch me.*
Cradled mango in the crown of his fingers,
rotated it clockwise,
softly pulling back the peel with his teeth,
sinking teeth and tongue into pale orange flesh
bite after bite without pause,
not even for the juice streaming down his hand, his arm
bite after bite until it was gone.
His eyes back on me, he smiled.
Delicious.
Couldn't move
as he lifted me up, carried me into the bathroom,
sucked on my lips, slipped off my dress and panties,
pulled me into running water,
soaping me,
soaping himself down, smiling, kneeling,
fingers and lips softly pulling labia apart,
head rotating in clockwise motion, sucking in juices,
lick after lick without pause until my thighs fluttered
and I moaned my electric explosion.
He stood up, then his
eyes were on mine, and he smiled.
Delicious.

Marks

Got a small scar on my left cheek—
looks like a moon crater. It is most
prominent when I smile. My son

had given me chicken pox.
Impatient, I nicked the purplish scab
while I healed.

Desiring perfection, I used to cover the scar
with foundation. It felt like a mask so
I poured that oily brown mass down the drain.

When I met my man, I envied his flawless skin.
Whenever I undressed in front of him, I wrapped
my arms around my waist to hide my stretch marks.

Then one night
before I could turn off the light
he wrapped blue and white ribbons around my hips
laid me down
slid down our sheets
stroked my navel
whispered that Black mothers
are Yemaya manifest.

When he brushed his lips down
and kissed
each of my crooked rivers
the Ogun
the Nile
the Limpopo
the Zambezi
the Niger
I knew not to covet
a child's soft smoothness.

We Were Cooking Sunday Dinner

Was reading a recipe aloud
to my honey-do
for vegetable stew.
Saw this article.

Had to read it.

Babe, I said.

Did you know
strawberries
blackberries
raspberries
are not really berries
but
watermelons
tomatoes
and eggplants are?

For real?
he said.

And
avocados
squashes
bell peppers
okra
olives
and pumpkins
are all fruits?

Makes sense, he said.
They have seeds.

Yeah, but they ain't as sweet
as a pineapple.

We laughed.

He walked up,
burrowing his nose into my neck from behind.

"The first five times I asked you out
you told me no.
My boys said you were bitter,"
He kissed me.
"But I knew better".

In two swift moves
my dress
was over my head
and I was on top
of the counter.

Don't move,
he whispered
as he walked back to the sink.

Babe, I said.
Those berries
are for the pie!

"Not anymore".

Honeymoon in Cerulean

I'm always going to cherish this,
our moonlit nights by quiescent waters
deep sea dives for starfish in red/orange/pink
and cerulean.

Some people have minatory, sclerotic hearts.
They will be invidious about our love, baby.
They will whisper. Cut their eyes at us.
Just because I can't stop holding your hand
or nuzzling your neck.

Why don't they get a room,
they will sneer,
as if four walls could contain my passion
for your lips and the way they purse when you call me to dinner
or yell my name in the heat of battle

or your resplendent scent--
Egyptian musk, lemon, parsley, and a modicum of sweat.
It's in our sheets and on my collar.

There will be men, coming to sample/savor your munificent juices;
women, coming for me to taste what would only be jejune.
We shall not let them. There's no place like home.

I will fight for us as long and hard as you do, honey,
in this paper chase. When we have children
run around for them and after them,
life can become languid, lachrymose
if we let it.

When we can't get away,
let us always look back on
these cerulean nights

Hard Candy

Grandma's candy dish
was like a bowl of love
I'd lift its top, and grab a couple of
hard candies.

Hard candies taught me patience.
Suck slowly. Relish the time
it takes to siphon inner juices
of cherry/lemon/lime.

When I got the last hard candy
I struggled not to gloat.
I'd let syrupy flavors
trickle down my throat.

I rush home every day now
lusting for nectarous lips like brandy
so I can kiss you slow, pull down your clothes
softly stroke hard candy.

I love the way you unwrap me
Like a chocolate covered treat,
I love to watch you watch me
as you lick me head to feet,

get in the steamy shower
rub aloe soap on skin
I get on my knees
pull you close and slip it in.

I suck the tip the way you like
You know how much you savor
The way I swallow every drop of
your ocean water flavor.

While you rest, I cook. We eat and talk.
Snuggle chest to chest.
Get hard candy ready.
Come where it's warm and wet.

Grab my hair as we thrust and moan
Nestle nipples between tongue and teeth.
I love my papa's candy, and us
sleeping wrapped up in our sheets.

Part IV | Goldstone

Freed Up

Like Gloria Steinem said
the truth will set us free but
first it will piss us off.

America better be glad
I love words, peace
as much as
I hate
throwing fists
and guns

You Can Find True Love in a Butterfly Cinquain

Justice
Pure water: all
Organic soil and food
All collars, colors: land. Home. Work.
Balance.
Time to meditate/meet/mingle.
Worship your God, your way.
Lay down all guns.
Concord

Divide
Categorize
Stereotype. Brainwash.
1 percent's foot, 99's necks.
Goad wars:
men-women, whites-non-whites, gays, poor
Kill unions. Laud bootstraps.
Loud media.
Discord

Haiku for Khari

Tying his sneakers
He wonders if tiny souls
Stitched laces and soles.

Aftermath of the Great American Celebration

The 6 train screeched into the station.
I spread my arms like a mother eagle
to keep drunken fools and tourists
anxious for a seat
behind my family.

The doors opened, my wall broken by shoving.
I eased into a seat, pulled my arms to my chest
to avoid foreign touch.

Tears trickled down my niece's cheeks like raindrops.
What's wrong, I cooed.

Somebody pushed me into a pole!

I scanned the crowd for supplicant faces. Finding none,
I announced: I wish I had seen the person who pushed you.
I'd have smacked them in the face!

My contralto mocked by laughter,
casual conversation, and the roar of wheels against tracks.

Yankee Girl Reverie

They say a lot of male mechanics dupe women, but not mine.
He is my sweet stand-in for Daddy.
I tease him. "You look like Harry Belafonte."
I look better, he quips, and we laugh.

I always get a hug and kiss on the cheek
before he asks what is wrong with my car and beckons for the keys.
You have a way to get home?

I could take a cab but I love the lilt in his voice.
I take the ride to keep him talking.
Today I ask,
What part of Jamaica are you from?

St. Mary's.
It's a lil country town.
It's quiet.
No chasing after ten o'clock.
There, you wonder where it is.

I nod, smile about my Some Day-
Caribbean sun browning/breeze licking my skin
mauve hibiscus nestled in the crook above my ear
bunches of Kiss Me Over the Gardens in purple drape over my hands,
evenings under the red thistle of the bottle brush tree,
a plate of callaloo and plantains
balanced on my knees.

Will you ever go back home to live?

No.
We all say we will but we don't.

As we drive past the delivery trucks and body shops along Route 22,
smoky air seeps through the windows--
I roll them up, clear my throat,
expelling the odor of progress.

The Unwelcome

They bequeath us haphazard mounds of muck.
Despite ginger steps, I once found myself
against a wall, scraping greenish feces
off my sandal,
cursing those honking geese.

As I marched past a group of goslings,
nibbling our newly planted grass, one
of the crèche pulled its neck erect.
Hissed.

Dodging smoldering cigarette butts, gum,
and bits of glass is quite enough.
Each day, each goose
leaves behind a pound of waste.

Research revealed methods to end this menace--
    an arrow through the body or blunt force;
    collies to inspire desperate flight;
    capture and transport to poultry processing plants;
    trapping, gassing, vehicular slaughter;
    pouring corn oil over the eggs to suffocate the embryos.

    Then again--
    so both can mind their young before they hatch,
    males and females
    shed the feathers that let them fly.
    Geese embrace monogamy in a way
    that humans have not—
    they stay with their mates for life.

One day my car was stopped in traffic by a line of geese--
one parent at the head,
goslings neatly in the middle,
other parent in back.
Despite my watch's insistent ticking,
I sat with my hands away from my horn.

Emergence

Vibrations--music, raindrops--motivate movement.
Us.
Earthworms.

As a little girl
after a hard rain
      I used to walk down the middle of the sidewalk
      so I wouldn't squish them.

      Giggled and squealed when the boys picked them up.
      Screamed, "Don't hurt them!"
      after we finished daring each other to rub their skins.

      Rolled my eyes at the bloody corpses
      left behind by the careless.

Cannot imagine life underground--
      I run up the stairs to escape the subway.
      Told my family to cremate me instead of buying a plot.

      All the burrowing earthworms do--
      aerating
      mineralizing soil
      so all we terrestrial creatures can grow.

Now, after a hard rain,
      I sometimes stop to watch them
      risk their lives on our sidewalks
      striding along, for the sensation of sun/air on skin

I step lively, but lightly

I Shouldn't Have Been There

My name is Jason Williams Jr. Here I stand.
In suit. Sharp haircut. With my parents--dignified.
My assailants, with a slap on the wrist.
In post-racial America.
I shouldn't have been there with my suitemates, at 17, them
wrestling me to the ground with bike lock around my neck,
them playing keep-away with the key.
They called me Three-Fifths and Fraction.
Bruised my lip when I fought back.
This room decorated with a Confederate flag and a pentagram.
In post-racial America.
Escaped home every weekend.
When my folks saw the Confederate flag and N-word scribbled on
a white board in my suite, they knew why. Filed a complaint.
Post-racial America.

Fellow students gathered around the arm-raised, black fisted
statues of Tommie Smith and John Carlos. To let me know I was not alone.
I came to San Jose State for an education. It was 2013.
In post-racial America.

And in 2016, an all-white jury found Colin Warren,
Logan Beaschler, Joseph "Brett" Bomgardner
guilty of "offensive touching". A misdemeanor.

A bike lock around my neck
calling me Three-Fifths and Fraction
scribbling the N word on a white board.
Not a hate crime, in post-racial America.

7-5 and 9-3 in favor of acquittal on the hate crime charges.
Beaschler claimed he hung the Confederate flag in support of states' rights;
the swastika, Nazi paraphernalia, "political satire."
In post-racial America?

One of the jurors who voted to acquit concluded: reasonable doubt
the two bike-lock incidents were driven by racial bias, though
the bullying that followed appeared racially tinged.

What is the verdict for black boys who beat up white boys in post-racial
America?

My assailants faced up to six months in jail, max.
Got community service sentence and 30 days in jail, served on a weekend
work program.
Post-racial America.

A woman juror in her 60s voted for conviction--
Beaschler, quiet and shy? Unaware displaying the Confederate flag was offensive to blacks?
She didn't buy it. "I never had a moment's doubt that they were guilty of hate crimes,".
Her statement should give me hope.
San Jose State formed a campus task force on racial discrimination, recommended:
increased diversity training for students,
more frequent visits to dorm rooms by staff
and a chief diversity officer.
Post-racial America.

Boycott

It is 2015. When my son wants to go out
I want to throw my body in front of the door.
Will a cop profile and search him?
My son could be taken out by a bullet.

I want to throw my body in front of the door.
Zimmerman got away with murder.
My son could be taken out by a bullet.
What else must black people do for equal protection under the law?

Zimmerman got away with murder.
We have a black president. He said, "Trayvon could have been me."
What else must black people do for equal protection under the law?
There is no post-racial America.

We have a black president. He said, "Trayvon could have been me."
Marissa Alexander almost got 20 years for standing her ground against her abuser.
There is no post-racial America.
Fuck Florida's beaches.

Marissa Alexander almost got 20 years for standing her ground against her abuser.
Fifty bullets at Sean Bell. Forty-one at Amadou Diallo.
Fuck Florida's beaches.
Stand Your Ground laws in 24 states. Strike them down.

Fifty bullets at Sean Bell. Forty-one at Amadou Diallo.
It is 2015. My son wants to go out.
Stand Your Ground laws in 24 states. Strike them down.
Will a cop profile and search my son?

For Jordan Russell Davis

We got one.

rap crap/thug music
bass/shaking cars
teen bravado

ten shots

10 whites, 2 blacks
a life sentence
Dunn: mortified over taking a human life

must be why he never dialed 911

Let them serve him cold pizza for lunch
blast Lil Rease in the chow hall/on the block
at least once a day,
and may Beef bounce off each wall of his cell
thrash his eardrums

Rondine of the Rhetorical Kind

Why did Scott dare run--cop and a gun at his back?
Why didn't he stop and drop to his knees?
Was it the hundreds hung from nooses on trees?
Some said wait 'til we have all the facts
before you say the cop shot because he was black.
Why do traffic stops on us, result in fatal attacks?
One bullet in the rear, one in the ear, 3 to the back. Fired with ease.
Why did Scott dare run?

Bell. Garner. Brown. Names, by the stack.
I too, have a son. Can someone tell me please,
is there a cure for America's fatal disease?
Slater in jail. Will a jury convict, based on the facts?
Or acquit, asking, Why did Scott dare run?

When a Plus Is Not

Sons of darker hue, my prayer is that you will never become one of
the New York Times' 1.5 million missing.

If you read Coates, Kunjufu, Madhubuti, Franklin, DuBois, Malcolm, King,
learn a skill, work, save, invest in socially responsible stocks, build a business,
vote,
speak standard English politely,
develop suited, stylistic savvy, it will never be enough.

Do not walk alone.
You may need a witness.
Do not walk in a large group.

Do not pull your hood over your head, even if it's cold.

Do not be tempted by fast money or guns; cells and caskets wait to claim
you.
Do not stand on the corner. Even if it's on your block.

If you must go to the bodega,
avoid the diabetic/hypertensive set-up:
quarter-waters, chips, cakes, sodas, Skittles.

If you are stopped and asked why you are anywhere/anytime
know that you will be told you look suspicious;
it is best to state you would like to remain silent.
They likely don't care to see your college or corporate ID.

Do not consent to a search if there is no warrant;
your voice must be even and calm.
Keep your hands visible.
Do not run by foot or by car;
it will not save your life.

If you are abused and get the badge number
file a complaint with the precinct
just in case someone ever cares about justice

I'll Be Damned

Decades of marching, pleading, voting, petitioning, rationalizing, and still it is
open carry for them, open season on us.

Teaching my son to bow his head
speak in soft tones when spoken to
leave his hoodies in the house
avoid darkened staircases
pull over
comply with commands
will not guarantee he won't become another
Kajuan Raye
Michael Sabbie
Keith Lamont Scott
Ezell Ford
Terence Crutcher
Alton Sterling
Philando Castile
Laquan McDonald
Akai Gurley
Charles Kinsey
Kalief Browder
Tamir Rice
Ramarley Graham

If they kill my
son
niece
cousins
sister
mother
aunt
uncle
friends
you won't see me
standing on stages
staring stoically into cameras
beatitudes of peace and mercy cascading from my mouth

Privilege

One of our ministers told a story this morning--
a white pastor asked why there are
so many churches in Harlem

How could a man of God wonder why we
would need pockets of refuge after fleeing a South
that beat/hung/chased us North
into overstuffed tenements
as earthly authorities, from the lowest to the highest, turned a blind eye

Why would we not need
to know Jesus looked like us
be reminded of God's love and mercy
by men/women who looked like us
so we could face another week of
earning a living on our knees

Why did we not deserve to
wear our best suits and dresses
have titles like
brother/sister/sir/ma'am/deacon/deaconess/usher
instead of
first names/boy/gal/darky/nigger/spook
as our children learned the Word and to
mind their manners
be told how pretty or handsome they looked
or applauded for performances and graduations

We raise(d) our own money for church buildings/support(ed) black-owned businesses
assist(ed) sisters and brothers in need with shelter/food/jobs/scholarships
and voted Adam into Congress
to raise hell and pass laws

If I could find that white pastor
I would ask him how Dylann Roof could walk into Emmanuel A.M.E.
ask to worship, kill nine members of its congregation,
and be offered forgiveness by the families of his victims

Hold

A command: "Hold the elevator!"
I heard a door slam and quickened footsteps.

Still smoldering about Eric Garner,
I almost pressed the Close Door button.

A young black man with my son's golden-brown complexion
walked in with his little sister.

I looked over his oval face framed by locs,
recognized he is a neighbor who always smiles, says, "Good morning."

He once looked at my Afro puff and asked me when
I planned to loc up.

Another day, he shared his plan to major in computer technology.
He does not smile today or speak.

As I got walked out on my floor, I almost blurted,
"I love you. Be careful out there."

Diaspora

The Chippewa called it Pewonigowink.
Stand by its banks at night with a flashlight.
Look for the white glow in the eyes of the walleye. Tapetum lucidum.

The son of the city manager caught a nine pounder once.
They've held a Walleye Festival in Flushing every year, ever since.
I hear they're "good for the table".

The walleye still live in the Flint River with all the chlorides.
Only 17 months of that water at the tap, and Kaylie screamed in the shower at the clump of hair in her hands.
His face was on the cover of Time; little Sincere still cries while his mother bathes him with bottled water. Ten dead from Legionnaire's.

The ignorant can claim innocence but officials had hundreds of years of history. From the writing of Dioscorides: "Lead makes the mind give way" to the "dangles" from lead type in the hands/feet of print shop workers in Ben Franklin's day.

A year before the switch back to Detroit's water:
Flint's GM plant stopped using city water to save car parts from corrosion.
Bottled water coolers in the state office building, but the tap water "was safe to drink".
No anti-corrosive chemicals to save the pipes from the Flint River.

Water warriors march with brown water in bottles. No politicians put in jail.
They get to allocate $80 million in federal aid, and it ain't enough to replace all the lead piping.

Will the walleye forever swim up the Flint River to spawn?
How many men in Flint will become impotent?

Chelation therapy flushes lead through urine. Does not undo damage to
axons, synapses, IQ.
Will the people of Flint get enough Vitamin C/calcium/iron/garlic/
cilantro/oregano?
Will Snyder give them 64 ounces of pure water per day to drink?
The Game/Cher/Diddy/Donny Wahlberg can buy only so much bottled
water.

No cure.
No end--20,000 killed and 2.5 million Nigerians displaced.
86 murdered in Dalori. Bullets and firebombs.

Bodies aflame:
Fire peels the epidermis, the dermis shrinks/splits leaking body fat.
Muscles dry out, contract, and the limbs sometimes move into
poses of agony: arched necks/backs.

Turns out body fat is good fuel.
Burned bodies fuel fear, and
Boko Haram/Flint officials understand
the cleansing properties of fire and water

No Access

The original route for Dakota Access Pipeline:
10 miles from Bismarck. If it were under construction there

and whites protested potential oil spills
in their water supply

would there have been sound cannons,
police in armored cars, dressed in riot gear, armed with assault rifles

cracks of batons/dog bites/mace/pepper spray,
faces swollen with red welts from rubber bullets wounds

strip searches, detention in dog kennels
numbers written in black ink on the arm.

Hillary--on her website anyway--will end environmental injustice,
clean up toxic sites, reduce asthma and lead poisoning for black and brown
children.

If she would heed Winona LaDuke she could call for
pipes for the people in Flint instead.

As lifelong fighter for women's rights
she could hunt down sex traffickers in the Bakken Oil Patch.

And not that anyone expected
she'd appear in the lobby of her Brooklyn headquarters

sit in the makeshift tipi with the Youth of the Standing Rock Sioux
Ghost Dance and sing Mni Wiconi to the heartbeat of Mother Earth

hug Tokata Iron Eyes as she wept over the police raid
and thank them for the letter demanding her support of the Water
Protectors

but to only say it is important everyone
respect the right to peaceful protest and for workers to do their jobs safely

in this time of the Seventh Fire, #iamnotwithher
no matter what beloved POTUS, FLOTUS, and Bernie say

about legacy, momentum,
going high when they go low.

Broken treaties and campaign promises
reek of blood and oil.

To Work

Some mornings after
running for the bus
up two flights of stairs
beating the green signal and closing doors
so I can grab a seat
and still my panting,
I see a body stretched out sleeping,
covered in sour/dirty layers,
taking up multiple seats,
I dash to the next car
so I can read or nap in peace
instead of covering my nose the whole ride.

Once, we all had to crowd into just a few cars.
We stood commiserating--
who to call or write to?
Those people must be put off the train.
Sometimes they urinate on the floor.
We work. Pay. Deserve comfort.

I think about these people sleeping
on those hard benches all night--
their names,
families,
what they did on their last jobs,
if they have mental illnesses or addictions
or if their landlords priced them out.

I wouldn't want to sleep with or fight
thieves or vermin in a public shelter either.

One of these mornings when I am standing up
I should remember to speak up:
for this system to work, not everyone can--
full employment is optimal at 4-5 percent unemployment,
or prices and interest rates go up.

Machines

As if discarded computers/cell phones/i-pods
televisions/digital cameras/CD and DVD players clogging up landfills;
fracking;
subway cars dropped to the bottom of the ocean
were not enough to keep me up nights
there is the
gold/tantalum/tin/tungsten
in our capacitors/resistors/circuit boards/vibration motors
in our computers/cell phones/i-pods/digital cameras.

On my computer, index finger clicking on the mouse
searching atrocities--5.4 million dead
2 million displaced in the Congo--
and which companies are in compliance
with Dodd Frank Section 1502;
auditing origins of tantalum/tin/tungsten.
How much is smelted/smuggled/sold,
and which gold is siphoned off into Swiss banks?

With fingers crossed, checked a compliance list--
red for low, yellow for medium, green for good.

My computer, green; cell phone company not listed.

Keeping my fingers crossed--
middle finger over index--
that my cell phone carrier is playing catch-up,

that children are not among those who dig into mud, through rocks,
filter water with finest mesh to be found,
inhale dust,
for gold/tantalum/tin/tungsten,
and that the women and men wear
protective clothes/boots/hardhats/helmets.

Do they earn enough to eat/pay rent/school fees for children?
Sleep enough after standing for hours in shallow water like Tantalus?

Fingers crossed that profits earned from my machines
don't buy the guns
that may or may not be waved over/at
the heads of women before they are raped in eastern Congo.

How many of my machines could I discard
if I discovered
my right index finger,
that answers calls/dials numbers/
taps out texts/opens the clasp of my sole gold necklace,
is tied to suffering?

Witness

America likes blacks and browns with hands over hearts and mouths so
beware if you are Baldwin's kind of black:
>sit or kneel during the national anthem;
>draw a lynching during school. write Black Lives Matter in response to a prompt
>to depict something you want to see come to an end;
>play video of your friend in a chokehold for the world to see;
>pass a law in the state legislature permitting the filming of police,
>record two black men pulled over by officers on your cell.
>Five cops for one man. Like he said, there's been too many killings.

Bader-Ginsburg says your kneeling is stupid.
A school counselor can refer you for a mental health assessment
>you will be interviewed
>>asked to sign a safety contract promising not to commit suicide.

You can be hounded until they find charges that will stick.

You can be Questioned: *have you been a cop?*
Until you walk in the shoes of a police officer you have no idea what's going on.
You're the type of person that will exploit this and cause chaos.
You are a race baiter, is what you are.
You will be accused of obstructing justice.

God, please fortify Colin's knee to spite the ground.
Keep little Tidiani Epps drawing and writing black historical rectitude.
Ramsey Orta said he was going to be okay,
but the brothers behind bars could not build a bulwark around him
as he served his sentence.
He is free. We know they will hound him.
Raise a parapet around us all.
May daniel pantaleo never hook his arm around another black/brown neck.
Watch over Little Rock, Rev. John Walker, and his mighty pen.
Ase.
Ase.
Ase.

Disclosure

I was here in this theater, shoulder to shoulder with my son for
Fruitvale Station and *12 Years A Slave*.
Wrangled with my twoness over *The Birth of a Nation*
    Snubbed *Get On Up*. Couldn't forgive James for Tammi Terrell.
    Spurned *Straight Outta Compton*. Couldn't forgive Dr. Dre or F. Gary Gray's silence on Dee Barnes.
    Cecily Tyson kept me from *Miles Ahead*.

Thought about my sister her freshman year, the night she and her friend hung out with their friends at Brother College past curfew, panicking as they looked for the exit that would help them avoid the R.A.s, and the group of men in a dorm room, pointing them this way and that, inviting them in to hide. My sister envisioned a train. Told her friend, "Girl, c'mon. Let's go."

That my sister could have been violated, then if she told, be poked, prodded, photographed, questioned about how many, why was she there, what was she wearing, what they said, how many times did she say no and how loudly did she say it, compelled to reveal sexual history, maybe be disbelieved, and I don't know how we would have managed to keep Daddy from strangling the perpetrators and any administrators trying to protect them.

Kept imagining Nate beckoning to Jean, to *come, get some of this.*

Wondering
        why the rape trial was news now, or if it would have been
        if Nate's accuser had been black, or if there been no Oscar buzz,
        kept me on the phone with friends and family, and up some nights.
Even though some folk are boycotting
this middle finger to D.W. Griffith
and I get why
I decided to be there for Nat, not Nate.
I was there because
        our prophet could have regaled in relative privilege as preacher
                but saw our freedom in an eclipse
        struck blows against our oppressors and got hung for it
        They let doctors dissect/de-skin/make grease/a purse of his body
                his great-great-great-great granddaughters,
            got his skull back in a box 185 years later.
Nyame Nnwu Na Mawu.

Sweater served as shroud as I wept over the speculum orum/the lash. Cherry Ann. Hark's wife.
Left the theater grateful for agency over my
> family
> gaze
> yeses and nos
> thoughts, and choice in tone as I speak them,
> labors with my hands, my back
> intellect and books.

It was not a perfect project:
> women were missing from surreptitious meetings
> and murder scenes
> the female slave who pinned her mistress so they could try to kill her too, omitted,
> but I am there for black art.

The industry is profit over people.
If we who believe in freedom show up,
prove a white savior is not requisite for a film to make money,
maybe, may be

Danny Glover can get Toussaint fully financed and finished.
We can see Hannibal/Mansa Musa/Queen Nanny/Prosser/Vesey/
Delaney/Wells-Barnett/The Mau Mau/Joan Little/Assata/Darren Seals/
Lavon Walker on screen.

We can glean history from books
but visual storytelling also stokes spirit.

I grieve for Nate's accuser. Wish somebody found her
before she swallowed almost 200 sleeping pills
and her son still had her by his side.

I pray for Nate
that as his daughters evolve into womanhood
he will choose to speak to young men about
        his 19-year-old self
        rape culture
        consent
        conscience

Part V | Jasper

Dear Yoko Ono

If woman is nigger of the world,
Then what am I?

For Osmel Sousa

Inner beauty ~~doesn't~~ exist(s).

~~That's something that unpretty~~
women ~~invented to~~ justify themselves?

Never.

Black Venezuelan women are ~~not~~ very beautiful...
Their noses? ~~are too big~~--
[N]o one ~~could~~ needs to operate on them!
~~Occasionally,~~ I choose a *morenita*
~~but she has to have a white girl's features--just painted dark.~~

Teal

"It's in this season," she said.
Pulled the shoe off the shelf.
Held it against my skin.
"Look at that, it's gorgeous with your skin tone."

Teal with gold threading. Sure was pretty.
I don't have anything that color in my closet, I said.

"You can wear neutral tops and bottoms and the shoes
for a pop of color. You know they don't make a lot of things for us."

I looked at her milk chocolate skin and wondered—
Is she just out to make a sale?

But it's true. I went to Ricky's a few weeks later. For lipstick.
Display case full of pale pinks. Loud reds, like for light bulbs
for those house parties after dark.

I asked the cocoa-brown salesgirl
if those were all the colors they had.
"Yes."
They don't make a lot of things for us, I whispered.
She nodded. "I know. We complain about it all the time."

Finally, at the Duane Reade in Harlem, found
a brown lipstick
pretty on my heart-shaped lips, against
my medium brown skin with golden undertones.

In the Moment

Emerged from the subway.
No bus.
Saw somebody coming out of a cab
on the corner.
Roof light was lit!

Waved.
Ran over.
Bent down to his open window.
Smiled, was about to speak my destination.

He yelled,
"Where are you going?
There is a lot of traffic!",
gesturing at the usual line of cars ahead.

A tingle in my spine. Heat on my neck.

For a moment, I wondered
if he would have yelled
had I been carrying a briefcase
instead of a purse
or was other
than black.

I looked at him. Stood tall. Said, "Never mind."

Walked back to the bus stop. Wondered.
Maybe English is not his first language, hence
the yelling.
But everyone understands a smile.

After I disembarked off the bus, huffed and puffed up the stairs.

Was marked 10 minutes late, but
signed my name in my most beautiful script.

For Bree Newsome

bashed air with my fist
when i saw her scale the pole

made mental lists of racist relics
i'd like to depredate. Inner Voice harrumphed:

how can u be brave
when u are scared of heights

Perceptions

Some perceive
loud
neck-rolling
finger-wagging
silky front-lace weave wearing
hair-snatching
uncultured
emasculating
know-nothing
big-bottomed caricatures.

Most unmarried/unwanted.
Mothering without fathers.

Canards cut.

Meanwhile
sesquipedalian and
sonorous,
we daughters of
Queen Nzingha
Nana Yaa Asantewaa
Sanite Belair
Sojourner Truth
Ella Baker
Diane Nash
Unita Blackwell
study macroaggressions/microaggressions,
soothe wounds of spirits.

Like Isis, for her Osiris, we
assemble mounds of flesh
mangled by bullets/billy clubs
denigrated from bully pulpits
to resurrect our husbands/lovers/brothers/
daughters/sons

But when we must mourn murder/maltreatment
we shout an orotund Esaw Garner
hell no
we will not forgive/forget
guns pointed at Recy Taylor's head in Alabama, 1944
that her daddy searched
husband/children wondered where she was
as six white men raped her.
The sheriff let them go.
Rosa Parks investigated/
initiated protests but there were no arrests.
Recy died at 97,
waiting
waiting
waiting
for justice.

We will not forgive/forget
Eleanor Bumpers, Rekia Boyd, Sandra Bland, Ralkina Jones,
Deborah Danner, Michelle Lee Shirley,
no knock warrants/battering rams/flash grenades
wrong addresses/itchy trigger fingers
or the policeman's bullet perforating Aiyana Jones' body
as she slept,
her grandmother witness to light leaving her 7-year-old eyes.

We will not forgive/forget
burgeoning bistros blocks away
from crumbling schools of color.

We will not forgive/forget
African girls forced into
marriage/motherhood
fistulas in lieu of school
or
that the surgery that can cure them came from
James Marion Sims who
kept African women--
Anarcha, Betsy, Lucy
on his property
as his property
to perfect his silver wire sutures without
anesthesia
for Anarcha, Betsy, Lucy.
Anesthesia
for Miss Ann.

We will not forgive/forget
that Boko Haram
has still not brought all
our beautiful girls back to Chibok.

Nevertheless,
sesquipedalian and sonorous,
we radiate joy.

The music of Stevie/Aretha/Marvin
motivates rhythmic motion of curves--
Rock Steady, baby.
Slicing/dicing/mincing
garlic and onions and peppers
for the right tang on tongue for collards,
through the peeling
of
peaches for cobbler,
stippling cinnamon/nutmeg/sugar
for banana pudding.

In our bedrooms
on bended knees
eyes closed
hands clasped, we beseech
on behalf
of diabetic mothers
hypertensive fathers.

Before we lay down to sleep
we are
yes, God, yes
soft on the
skin
on the mouth
in the mouth.

Because many of we
sesquipedalian
sonorous sisters have
waited by windows for spiritually broken fathers/mothers/significant others,
had unwanted touches/pinches/punches/penetrations we were to tell no one about,
beauticians and mamas frowned up, raking our kinky hair
       with combs that had teeth too small,
fingers pointed at skin that was too black to be beautiful,
had wages beneath our worth,
we
embrace those of us who neck roll/
wave fingers.

We know that once
our sisters learn
self-care
self-love
they will
lift as they climb
towards boardrooms,
to burrow their heads in

The Bluest Eye,
to poem, like Rita Dove,
to rule over courtrooms like Loretta Lynch,
teach our children to question why the American Dream
is a nightmare for many,
to calculate the dimensions of the pyramids,
study how to cure cancer,
fight like Maxine Waters,
(Hands off Assata!)
place a #blacklivesmatter placard
in Aniah Ferguson's flailing arms,
(put that on worldstarhiphop)
and join our allies to fight for
lower college tuition
jobs for all
and vote to
displace the shrinking
white supremacist 1%.

But canards cut.

For Sista Gaines

maybe our millennial moses
was thinking about freddie gray
as she was riding along on her freedom train--
shackles around his wrists and ankles,
unbelted/ head first/on his belly in a police van,
distress to his neck/spinal cord,
the way his legs dragged along on the ground,
what he was thinking before he took his last conscious breath.

Not me. Not today. Not ever.

can't forget her strident demand
that they identify themselves,
produce a delegation of authority order
because she didn't participate in their system,
her demand they return the keys they snatched from her ignition,
that there is no crime, no victim here,
you're not going to steal my car.
These bitches going to see a fight today. Fuck that.
commanded five-year-old Kodi: *Fight they asses*
if they tried to remove him from the car.
Kidnapping me? kidnapping my kids?

I promise you, you will have to murder me.
Listen. I've never been to jail and I never will go.
They will have to kill me in front my children.
You guys will have to take me away from here in a body bag.
Look me in my eyes.
I'm not scared of ya'll.
I'm gonna sue your asses.
I'm not gonna comply to ya'll criminal fucking ways. I'm not going to do it.
You see these fucking rebels? They live on forever.
Where's the delegation of authority order? He doesn't even know what it is.
Ya'll plotting on a fucking woman.

told kodi to record her arrest.
You fight them. You see what they do to us.
He's seen videos of you shooting people who look like his father. uncles.
Of course, I won't raise submissive-ass fucking children.

the officers were calm, polite, soft-spoken
but what can you do when you want to opt out
from this unjust just-us system
and you can't get videos of black larruped bodies out of your head

when they came for her on august 1
for misdemeanors:
operating an unregistered motor vehicle,
driving without current tags,
driving an uninsured vehicle,
failure to display registration card on demand
driving a vehicle on a highway with a suspended registration.
resisting/interfering with arrest
disorderly conduct,
disturbing the peace
littering

some say it was the lead she inhaled/ingested at
West Belvedere, or
the miscarriage she blamed on her arrest
that compelled her to keep Kodi and Big Girl by her side

nobody knows if police ever played the message her daddy made for her
or if they had allowed her mama try to talk her into surrendering
Kodi's cheek would have the mark of her lipstick instead of a bullet wound

maybe she would have finished her political science degree at Morgan State.
wonder if she'd have drawn kohl around her perfect oval eyes
worn a dress, or eyeshadow, of Blue and Orange
to contrast the black of her gown.

marilyn mosby tried; freddie's murderers are free.
maybe korryn was thinking about her kodi all along
as she clung to him, to Big Girl, thinking,
"Be free, or die a slave"
when the bullets hit

you see these fucking rebels?

they live on forever,
and korryn's baby daughter drinks ersatz
in lieu of mother's milk.

Movement

Sometimes being the first anything doesn't mean shit.

Even though it had been Earth Day on April 22, 2015, and
a black woman gave birth to us all,
and three black women--Alicia Garza, Patrese Cullors, Opal Tometi--
 founded #BlackLivesMatter,
only 30 or 50 or 100
black/brown/white somber faces at Union Square
protesting for Rekia Boyd and other black women victims of police brutality.
I'd have been with them--was at another meeting
with black/brown/white brothers and sisters,
melding ideologies for an organizational mission statement.

Every now and then, wonder if more would have marched for Rekia
if her murder had been on video, but knowing
Trayvon's was on audio and thousands marched for him
been telling myself the rain on that day kept people away.
Is it #genderbias? Do people think our black girls and women are less
endangered than our men?
That we women are strong enough to stand on our own?

We all black girl magical,
iron may sharpen iron, but even iron wears out.
For the sake of our Dajerria Bectons, we don't have time for excuses,
benign neglect,
with our black daughters getting tossed like,
some have said, rag dolls.

At least rag dolls are cherished.
Collected.
Cradled.
Given as gifts.
Placed on shelves with care.
Not thrown out of a desk and dragged
lifted and body slammed, bruised,
vision blurred, a concussion from head hitting the floor.

On the Mend

Quenepas.
My first love called them quenepas. He kissed my nipples like my lips. Softly.
They plumped into perfect orbs. He would stop. Sit back to admire them as I squirmed.
My breasts feeling as beautiful as they looked in the mirror.

But he moved on. The next asked me to marry, left two weeks before I gave birth.
So he would grow healthy and strong, the nurse stood by as I sat sorely on stitches, gently placing right, then left nipple in my son's tiny mouth.

They went flat. Inverted nipples, was what they told me.
When they took him to the nursery, they fed him by bottle.
Second night, they served dinners for two and sparkling cider--
I only used one of the glasses.

My roommate's husband held their daughter.
Daddy's girl, Daddy's girl, he cooed.
Muffled my failure/tears with a towel. Wished my father was there to coo
Daddy's girl, Daddy's girl;
 he was home building the crib.

Tried pumping. Teaspoonfuls in bottle, the rest leaking. Soaking through shirts. Back to formula.
At three months, son's skin turned scaly: eczema. Cousin suggested relactation.
Breast is best. Dry, painful suckling/wet cries for bottle.

Watched as friends/family breastfed. Descendant of original Earth Mother/
enslaved wet nurses--should this not come naturally?

Undressed alone in front of my mirror. Ogled my breasts. Symmetrical.
Plump--like quenepas.
From every angle. Beautiful.

Why did they only cradle son through story time? To sleep?
 His asthma: my fault. Surrendered the struggle too soon. Breast is best.

Wish I'd had the internet then. Might have learned inverted nipples are
common for first time babies. Could have found the Hoffman technique for
nipple inversion--he could have "enjoyed helping to draw them out"--had
son's father stuck around.

But what if all that sucking and pleasurable pulling hadn't worked?
Had no more babies to see if my beautiful breasts could serve biological
purpose.

Lactivists lambaste public shaming of breastfeeding mothers
but who posts and blogs against bottle shamers for women like me?

Son is a man now.
And my nipples still plump into perfect orbs with the proper kiss.
But I am undoing damage:
To reverse years of rounding shoulders in shame, I train myself to
thrust them back for my bosom's resplendent display.

An Ode to Panetta and Wannett

If i were strong, or Catholic,
in lieu of
briskly tapping fingers
against kissing thighs,

i would be still/stoic like
Saint Agatha as she
proclaimed her faith against iron pincers
and held her severed breasts on a platter.

No, no, the technician gently scolds.
You have to keep still.

My eyes fixed on the ceiling.
No patterns to distract me as
one plate descends
to flatten my breast
against a metal one.

As i am sandwiched and photographed
i play a round of $100,000 Pyramid so i won't
imagine my breasts popping like balloons.

Things i have pressed--
time
garlic
clothes
a receiver against my ear
my head against a lover's chest
my hair, before i knew better.

She tells me i have dense breasts and
will probably need an ultrasound too.
She shakes her head resignedly.

The things we women must do.

Thank God for that technician
because that form letter
stated there was a finding.

Brushed it off at first
But then i began to wonder how would i tell my family?

i am only 41
my son, 18, still needs me.

What about work and bills?

Single or double mastectomy?
Plastic surgery?
Radiation? Chemotherapy?
What kind/color wig would i wear
as i lose my hair?

i called my doctor.
She said They didn't find anything, and
the radiologist needs an ultrasound for a clearer picture.

And,
 i say, when I get to the clinic,
a different form letter.

They say, They know.

But I know they won't write a new one.

I could.
Just for dense-breasted women like me.

Ultrasound.
On the table, shivering when the cold gel fell.
More pressing. A wand, this time, against my dense breasts.

All she saw was a benign cyst
that might go away on its own.

Less painful than the mammogram.
I am relieved.
I can do the ultrasound instead!

No, you need both.
The mammogram can catch things
like calcifications that the ultrasound cannot.

Thought my dense breasts
couldn't/wouldn't allow Them to see?

Not only must i explore/memorize
the "architecture" of my breasts but
do both exams every year?

Are lives saved
and/or risks increased?
Experts do not agree, online.

Should mammograms be done
every 2 or 3 years
from the ages of 50-69?
Yes? No? Yes? No? Yes? No? Yes? No?

The things we women must do.

Absolution

Every woman must have a room of her own but
what about a womb?

Since you offend me should I not let them cut you out?

I.
You nourished and brought me my son, but
six years ago, betrayed me--
Two days a month of runny blood.
Clots like clumps of scarlet jelly.
Belly of a fourth month pregnancy.
Anemia. Headaches. Dizziness. Weakness. Burning lower back pain.

Told my GYN--hysterectomy, out of the question.
It has been alleged to wreck the sex drive.
Every option she offered seemed capable of sucking away life force:
Lupron, that could deplete my bones.
Surgical removal: could lead to heavy bleeding and emergency hysterectomy.
Endometrial ablation,
Uterine embolization--an end to childbearing.

Went a natural route instead:
Abstained from alcohol.
Veganism. Iron pills.
Taheebo and yellow dock teas.
Exercise. Yoga, then
Acupuncture once per week, bitter Chinese herbal tea every morning, night for six months.

Talked to other sisters about their fibroid journeys:
surgical removal; others, hysterectomies.
Ruminated over why we Black American women are so afflicted?
Has 500 years of the trading block infected our melanin? DNA?

II.
When the bleeding was every day for half a month,
clots the size of a liver.
Three, two, then one birth control pill a day to stop the flow.
fibroids multiplied: one pedunculated, one the size of a grapefruit,
bradycardia: heart rate dwindled to 37 beats per minute.
Uterine fibroid embolization.
Heavy cramping, pain in legs for a week
no more babies but periods eased. No headaches.
Heart rate normal. Energy. Exercise.

III.
Two years later there I sat, afraid
to move, to drip more of me.
Wiped myself off the toilet seat. Bathroom floor and door.
Blew the dust off Queen Afua's Sacred Woman.
Thumbed through for answers, and
It is I who betrayed you.

I apologize for
constricting your circulation with jeans and pants most falls and winters
not learning to play the shakere
not arising at dawn for sacred baths
not anointing my head, third eye, womb with frankincense
not pouring libations to Florence, James, Lena, John, Pauline, Sallie, Boston, Joan, Melvin
not placing an orchid in my bedroom and an aloe vera plant in my front window
keeping my ankh in my jewelry box
not building an altar graced by moonstones/turquoise/fresh flowers/a bowl of water/
fresh oranges/apples for the ancestors
not putting a feather on a pedestal
not sprinkling lavender on my forehead, heart, on you
not reciting the 42 laws of Ma'at at dawn and dusk
not praying every morning midday evening nighttime

not meditating
not fire breathing
not thinking and speaking positively and kindly at all times
not begging your mercy for the men cleansing themselves of their negativity in, through me/you
not seeking enough solitude and silence
not keeping a journal solely for you
not forming a sacred womb circle with my sisters.

I promise to:
Grow the willpower to acquire, and do, what you require.
Choreograph and cavort a free-flowing dance under the arch of Nut.

I hope my rose quartz caresses earn your forgiveness.

Accountable Talk

Two girls, 12 and 13, raped
in a school auditorium.
When the story hit the papers,
in lieu of the usual shake of the head and, "what a shame"
a teacher gathered her eleven and twelve-year-olds to talk.
Most of them, boys and girls—
said the rape was the girls' fault.
It must have been what they were wearing.
Why did the girls go into the auditorium with the boys?
The lack of sympathy/empathy
brought the teacher to tears, and counselors in to talk--
afterwards most of the boys and girls
still blamed the victims.
Those of us who care are left
to wonder when the grown folk
will get together and get it together
because our children
are watching
listening
learning

Trigger Alert

We meant well.
Didn't shush NeeNee's long stories,
her singing when she found her alto-soprano.
Always let her choose--
Which book? The pink or purple skirt? Dress? Blouse?

One of the few don'ts: talking to strangers.
Because she listened,
one from a carful of men asking her and her friends
where the college party was got out of the car.
Stuck his hand in his pocket.
Motioned the pulling of a trigger.

They fled.
My niece, on her knees.
Hiding. Behind a car.

A man in the neighborhood saw.
Stayed until their friends picked them up.
Lucky.

Wish somebody had been there

> to block Taijae Edwards's punch before
> > he broke a girl's jaw for refusing his kiss;

> to stop Joyce Quaweay's boyfriend from stripping her naked
> > handcuffing her to a bench and beating her to death
> > in front of her children because she would not submit.
> > He sat on the stoop of the house.
> > Told the cops, "I'm the one you want."

> to pull Reginald Moise off Tiarah Poyau before he could grind on her.
> > shoot her through the eye during Jouvert last weekend
> > when she said *Get Off Me.*

Amidst all this misogynoir
thought I was doing a good thing when
I spread dozens of books on triumph over tragedies on desks.
Invited students to peruse them all.
Take notes on interesting titles.

Kay said Miss, I was interested in *Lucky*
but she gets raped
and that's too much.
You should have put a trigger alert on this one.
Somebody might have gone through that.

Paused before I replied.
Proud. Hate to be wrong but saw the light.
Said, I'm sorry, you're right.
Thanks for telling me.
I will do that next time.

Wish I had thought to add:
Baby girl. I hope that wasn't your experience.
Do you need to talk?

If the man
who called me a slut and a bitch
for refusing to go to his house
for our second date
had trigger alert
written across his forehead there wouldn't have been a first date
for him to put his arm around me,
draw me into his peruvulent chest to inhale baby powder/cologne,
to let me rest my head, and
lull the corybantic inner noise
about bills and being
the brave one at the helm.

Stroking

I.
I was reading aloud to my students the other day.
Saw the movement of a hand in my peripheral vision.
Two of my girls. Both pretty. Friends.
They coordinate their bathroom trips.

One, Asian-American, is forlorn, again
with head on desk, in her book,
and the other, African American, sitting across from her
slowly stroking her friend's silky black hair as she reads along.

II.
Although A Thousand Splendid Suns had me, us, deeply engaged,
    I thought about our black girls.
    Seen plenty in rage/pain--
    over verbal and physical assaults
    problems at home, or with love.
How many black girls
with kinky/nappy 4b/4c hair
get comforted by someone stroking it lovingly?

Without even looking up, I wondered
if this young sister had the same
longing in her eyes, like
me in elementary school,
in line behind white or Latina girls who had straight
hair hanging down their backs.

Never wanted to be other than black,
but oh, if my great-great-great (wherever it was) grandmother's Cherokee blood
or great-grandfather's mulatto genes
had been a little stronger.

Not that my hair has never been touched by hands
other than mother, cousin, hairdressers.

But it was out of curiosity--
        Like that summer in Boston
        one of seven black people in a pre-college program
        An Asian-American girl gazed at my cornrows
        and asked if she could touch my hair.

I consented, hoping for understanding,
but she rubbed my braids with her fingers
like she was petting a strange animal in a zoo;

Or sexual arousal:
It's been pulled during sex, never stroked after.

But there was one brotha
who didn't have much money
but he took me to Battery Park to watch the sunset
sat me on a bench
guided my head to his lap
gently coiled his fingers around my two-stranded twists
and I lay there for the longest time.

III.
In lieu of more YouTube tutorials and blogs
    celebrating nappy black hair beauty
        what we could use, is some stroking.
            No one should take 40 years to fall in love with her
            own hair.

IV.
I am projecting pain, perhaps.
Maybe this was just one girl soothing another
But if the black girl was the one hurting
would her friend have stroked her hair
so she wouldn't have to cry

Connections

When I said she had the highest grade,
she ran over. Hugged me tightly.
I asked,

Why do you always wear that hat and hood?
Why are you hiding?

"I don't like my hair yet."

Let me see.

She crouched by my desk
eased off her navy blue wool hat
to reveal
a teeny-weeny afro.

I looked at her--
eyes like black pearls.

That's beautiful.

Get yourself a cute pair of earrings.
Lipstick/lip gloss.
Wear them.

"Miss, I am insecure--,"
her fingers brushing her cheeks--
"I have acne."

I had that too.
I know what it's like.

But you have to walk down the street,
the hallway
like you're the finest thing on two feet.

"Even if I don't feel that way?"

Especially when you don't.

Confidence will make you
even more beautiful.

She smiled,
thanked me,
went back to her seat.

Remembering the tan wool coat
I hid beneath and sweated through in class
    at 15,
when my friend came in to say
she too had been in her room, to chat,
I said, let's take her shopping
for cute clothes,
    earrings to embellish her ears.

Yeah, we said, so

beautiful Jasmine,
    fragrant flower,
might embody her name,
    stop rushing past mirrors, and
sashay like Carmen Jones
    past admiring and jealous eyes alike

Resistance

Yeah, girl. Natural 26 years.
You should have seen me on 125th street: wide grin, erect neck, and spine.
Another African sister asked if I wanted my hair braided.
I said, "No thank you,".
Off I went in my wooly wonderfulness, hips and thighs rocking and rolling.

Was in too much of a hurry to tell her why extensions and I are done:
a braider spilled hot water on my neck when she was dipping the ends of my braids
the itchiness and the "black girl pat"
stiff shoulders from hours of detangling Kanekelon hair out of mine,
my hairs wrapped up in the braids on the floor, their bulbs sticking out from the roots.

I didn't find her until I was 40, but I have a sista who gently
twists, braids, or coils the hair that grows out of my head.
Finally love every 4b/4c strand God/Goddess gifted me--except the grays.

No matter how long, how often my hairdresser skillfully slathers
henna/permanent black dye in my hair
one gray hair coarsely taunts me at one temple.
Those color touch-up brushes that look like mascara wands
kidnap my hair into their bristles, so every six or eight weeks, there I am,
black dye slathered in my hair so one gray hair can taunt me again from one temple.
I hear there is color spray on the market, but it costs.

When I am 60, no, 70, well, one day
gonna let this silver shimmer
like the sterling earrings, bangles, and rings I will wear to match.

Redress

Angela. Wish I knew how,
where to find you.
Would you remember me, or that I sat behind you
in our eighth grade English class?
As we discussed Animal Farm, other works of the
Eurocentric canon, I studied the
swell
twirls
twists of
your two neat plaits.

You were the only one of us who hadn't been
seated
bent at the nape of the neck
by the stove in her mother's kitchen
or in Mrs. Johnson's salon
hot comb
Dax
Blue Magic
Ultra Sheen
or
Dark and Lovely Creme relaxer
scorching her coils into submission.

Fed up with your confidence
in revealing
kinks and kitchens
our mothers tried to hide,
I asked you,
"Why don't you straighten your hair?"

I remember your smile.
You turned around, announced,
"my hair doesn't need to be straightened"
and turned back to your work.
"Yes, it does," I snickered.

I wish you had been there to see me

at 18
when I heard Farrakhan accuse
sisters and brothers
who "do things" to our hair
of being dissatisfied
with the way God gave it to us.
I was angry until
I realized my shame of its texture
and determined to never chemically alter it again,

the day I walked down 125th Street,
scarf secured around my head,
strands springing forth,
wrapped around each other like
the roots of a mangrove,
when an African sister offered to braid my hair.
I smiled through my no thank you,
eyes affixed on the horizon
when she asked, "You're going to wear your hair like that?"

at 40 when I undid my last box braid,
threw away my last
plastic bag full
of unraveled Kanekalon hair

at 46 when the last comb infiltrated my crown.
I wish you could see me work
my scalp,
my hair over with
witch hazel, water, peppermint oil.

At 48, locs caress my shoulders.

Yesterday, a little girl looked up at me,
my locs framing my face.
She said, "You look pretty. I like your hair,".
It is what I should have said to you that day in class,
though you never needed me to.

How Far We've Come

According to my Newsfeed
the word no
can earn a woman a body bag
these days

You could be enjoying yourself with friends in a bar
a man flirts
you turn him down, and
when you leave to go home to your three children
he shoots you in the chest
because you said no again

We teach our daughters to say no
to bad touches, even
encourage them to learn how to shoot guns themselves
if they want
they could join the Army
serve in Iraq
but if your daughter
says no
to becoming one of three women sexually assaulted or raped in the military

she could be found with bruises
scratch and tooth marks
eye hanging from a socket (like Emmet Till)
broken nose
several teeth knocked back
military gloves glued to her hands
acid burns on her trigger finger and inner thighs
"corrosive material poured" on her vagina
pistol-sized bullet hole through the left side of her head
      (she was right-handed)
her death ruled a homicide, then a suicide, by M-16 in her mouth
(40-inch weapon; she was 5'1)

#SayHerName: Janese Talton-Jackson, 29, January 22, 2016
#SayHerName: Private LaVeda Lynn Johnson, 19, July 2005

Child's Play

she is pretty, brown, 20 years old
squeezes her plump frame into too-tight clothes
all day she wanders in and out of classes or the hallway
failing everything

just like last year, she hangs on the arm of her boyfriend
while he does his work
and she neglects her own

if i thought she would listen
i would speak to her, woman to woman,
tell her that no man likes a hanger-on
with empty hands and dreams for long

i told her boyfriend i was worried
he said, miss, I try to tell her
to pass and graduate too.
She doesn't listen.

if i thought she would listen
i would tell her, woman to woman
eventually her arm
that is locked around his
will feel like an anvil

She Hid It Well

Was chatting with my colleague. It was almost 3:00.
Was about to get my coat when I saw a face in the door.
I summoned her in.

Baseball cap sat low on her head,
heavy-lidded eyes, like she hadn't been to sleep.

Ready for clichéd excuses and promises to pass,
I smiled patiently.

Where have you been, I asked as she sat down at a desk.
Miss.
It's life.

Is everything OK at home?

She shook her head.
My boyfriend hit me.

I scanned her golden-brown skin for bruises.
Intelligent, pretty, and 18. Usually cheerful.
My colleague hung her head. We had no idea, all this time.

I eased next to her, held her shoulder gently.
Let her lean on me to cry.

Are you still with him?
No. We been together since I was 14.

Is he stalking you?
She shook her head.

Just feeling stress and depression. No hope.
Does your mother know?

No.
You have to tell somebody.

The social worker wants me to see a counselor.
Are you going to?
She shook her head.

You should.
Therapists are trained to deal with these situations.
(Unlike me)

You don't have to be ashamed.
Sometimes we fall in love with people who are wrong for us.
It happens. I know women who have been abused.
At least you got away.
It could have been worse.

You should tell your mother.
Yes, she will get angry--that is what we do.
But it is only because she loves you.

Do you have any older brothers?
She nods.
Girl, tell them too.

I left to get our counselor
while my colleague talked to her.

We hugged her. Said, "We're here for you."
Watched her retreat down the hall.

Flashed back to my first and only time:
My boyfriend put his finger in my face, pushed my head back.
I chased him, grabbed the pillow off his bed,
hit him in the eye with all my 16-year-old rage.
How lucky I was--he didn't come after me with all
6 feet and 180 pounds.

I wanted to take her home, cook her a meal,
let her sleep soundly but
I have no room

Sisterhood (for Tanya)

When you fall into muck and mire
They bathe you in words that inspire.

Blow specks and planks from each other's eyes
Rumors about the other are phenomenal lies.

They pick you up when you fall off the path,
unkind acts will earn their wrath.

They've scratched and oiled your scalp
Combed and braided your hair.
Secrets laughed and gasped about
but never ever shared.

Sorrow bursts through your door, they stand up for hours
rinsing, chopping, dipping meats in cornmeal and flour.
Invite you over for a bite to eat.
Joke to hear you laugh, listen as you weep.

Read your writing, nudge you
to beautify what ebbs from every nib.
Every woman needs a sisterhood
that will stick to the ribs.

This Is Why I Smile at My Friend Soraya

"This is the last piece I'll play.
I learned it on my own."

And
she sits there on her stool
hair brushing her shoulders
like a mother's loving touch,
fingernails painted pink
strumming her guitar
lips pursed
eyes fixed on her sheet music.

The song is short
but in my head, it lingers

Love Letter

My Dear Sisters,

When a bigot takes to Instagram: "Black women will never be
 as beautiful as white women"

No need for clapbacks about surgery/lip filler/Angelina
Jolie on a pedestal.

A confident woman does not extol her virtues to any one who does
not love her.

She will complement mahogany skin with lips in perfect purple
pulchritude

strap on heels/slip on sneakers and step.

When a bigot takes to Instagram:
"Black women will never be as beautiful as white women"--
No need for clapbacks about surgery/lip filler/or Angelina on a pedestal.
A confident woman does not extol her virtues to any one who
does not love her.
She will complement mahogany skin with lips in perfect purple pulchritude.

No need for clapbacks about surgery/lip filler/Angelina Jolie on a pedestal.
Strap on heels/slip on sneakers, and step.
She will complement mahogany skin with lips in perfect purple pulchritude.
The fuller the lips, the bigger the orgasm.

Strap on heels/slip on sneakers, and step.
They already know--
The fuller the lips, the bigger the orgasm.
And black matches everything.

They already know--
The human race runs the gamut of shades,
And black matches everything.
Slick on cayenne pepper red lipstick if you want to: the brighter, the better.

The human race runs the gamut of shades,
A confident woman does not extol her virtues to any one who does not love her.
Slick on cayenne pepper red lipstick if you want to: the brighter, the better, when a bigot takes to Instagram: "Black women will never be as beautiful as white women".

No/need/for/clapbacks/about/surgery/lipfiller/Angelina/Jolie/on/a/pedestal/a/confident/woman/does/not/extol/her/virtues/to/anyone/who/does/not/love/her/she/will/complement/mahogany/skin/with/lips/in/perfect/purple/pulchritude/strap/on/heels/slip/on/sneakers/and/step.

Thank you, Amber Rose

Tyrese:"The comfortability that some people find in wanting to touch or grope you ... It's an energy that's being sent out there that creates that type of response."

I was wearing jeans, a shirt,
sneakers, and my varsity jacket,
brotherman asked if I had a
subway token,
I said no,
he pulled out his switchblade,
commanded: Don't you scream.
Searched my pockets for cash,
found none,
pointed his switchblade forward.
Move.
He looked me up/down.
Wait.
He backed me up against the wall.
I want to make it with you.
Please don't.
Please, I gasped,
stomach knotting/churning.

Wasn't tears
tender age
that stopped him but fear
somebody might appear in that
empty station.

With a wave of the switchblade-
Walk.

As we ascended the stairs:
What's your name?
Soon as we hit daylight, I ran.

Before you ask why I was there
unescorted,
at 17
a snatch of privacy is hard to come
by
for a girl with watchful parents
and a house of open doors.
Was just waiting for a guy that I
loved to kiss
because:
he grinded my hips against his
while I sucked the underside of his
upper lip
and had "comfortability"
with
No

Rev Run: "Dress how you want to be addressed."

You would never admonish
Trayvon's father
for his son's sartorial choice;
hope you might be as
understanding
about my
Girls' Night Out--

I was in a crowded club.
A man asked me to dance.

First song:
small talk about our names
him being from Long Island
me being dangerously beautiful.

Don't know what it was about my
simple blazer, blouse, jeans, and
boots
that made him think he could then

lock arms around my breasts
slide his hands towards my crotch
nuzzle his face in my hair

Not wanting to surrender my spot
on the dance floor
at first,
I pushed off/pulled his arms
then had to yank myself away.

He saw me later.
I said,
The way you touched me made
me uncomfortable.

"If I can't touch you, I can't dance
with you."

Had this happened to your wife
or one of your daughters,
would you console/question/
blame
or are they not allowed to have a
Girls' Night Out

Kanye West

If somebody
mailed in a headshot
of Kanye's
mahogany-skinned mama
when she was young
For This Casting Call:
Season 4
Multi-racial women
only
No Make up
please
come as you are
Jack Studios
Studio 6
601 West 26th Street
New York, NY 10001

would it have
come back
labeled
RETURN TO SENDER

Multi-racial women only

Objectified

Trick Daddy
driving around talking about
Spanish hoes and white hoes
getting finer than a motherfucker.
If they learn to fry chicken
us black hoes
will be useless
unless we tighten up.
Daniel Holtzclaw
driving his police cruiser around poor neighborhoods,
picking on black women:
sodomizing and raping
compelling fellatio at gunpoint
because he thought no one
would notice.
Chasm between them two ain't exactly river deep.

Part VI | Jade

Perigee Moon

On this eve of
the super moon
menstruating
meditating about
Muslim student at UMichigan
pulling off her hijab
so a white man
would not
set her
on fire
with a lighter

250 moons ago, as fresh
college grad
used to chat with one of the black guards who liked my gele
when I worked at the Museum of Natural History
It shows your pride in your culture
White supervisor made me
take it off
No hats
Worried I would be fired
I complied

Every day
especially after that day
as I passed by the Equestrian Statue of Theodore Roosevelt
imagined the African man
Native American man
pushing Teddy
off his horse
riding off into the sunset

Even in 2012
an Upper West Side resident
campaigned
to have that racist symbol removed.
The city said
No.
Museum spokesman Michael Walker:
It belongs…art…historical tradition…equestrian statuary
artist…depict exploration

On this eve of
the super moon
menstruating
meditating
Don't know if
there are enough
safety pins
groups of 300 to walk our Natashas to class but
tomorrow Mother Moon
will be brighter
closer
As the skies darken
I will stand outside
look up
imbue myself in healing light

Will Love Trump Hate?

We have embalming fluid. We should stop leaving flowers
for the dead if they were murdered.

Injustice reeks,
floral scents too faint.

First flowers for Will Sims
dried out, drooping, if even still there.

Who will nudge fresh ones through the gate?
Does anyone light the candles at night?

How many times did his attackers call him a nigger
as they robbed and beat him?

What was he thinking
before he closed his eyes for the last time on the side of the road?

Looked for his music on YouTube to hear him on piano and guitar--
the only Will Sims I found is white.

Psychological study showed black boys
perceived as older than they are, less innocent; naturally

William Pulliam is 62, unapologetic that he killed
15-year-old James Means for bumping into him.

The flowers at James's funeral must have been beautiful but
injustice reeks, floral scents too faint.

Does Jordan Jackson fight sleep because he dreams
flying mulch, countless rows of cotton, his body hitting concrete,

the snap of his arm breaking, his four-year-old sister's cries?
His mother will home school them from now on.

Punched by a white man who perceived *mugger*
who would rob his wife as they sat in their car,

Chase Coleman got knocked back 10 feet,
landed on his bottom. Quit cross country track.

Lately, I've been giving white folk
wide berth in public spaces.

More black folk buying guns these days. Held a 45 once.
Hard, heavy in right hand. Couldn't imagine aiming at anyone and pulling the trigger.

But was thinking: Learn to stand your ground. Kill.
Sidestep seeping blood. Buff surfaces fingers have touched. Sleep through the night.

But two young white women were on the train
leaning over the poster board across their laps

Colored pencils in hand they drew: LOVE TRUMPS HATE.
They got off at Union Square with dozens of others, all colors, to join the anti-Trump march.

A thousand people, all colors, wearing Run With Chase t-shirts, ran a Fun Run.
Chase Coleman smiled through his victory lap.

Thousands of dollars, from all colors, raised for the Go Fund Me campaigns for Jordan Jackson, James Means, Will Simms.

White grandmother texted an invitation to Thanksgiving dinner to a black boy
by accident. She said he could come over anyway.

That's what grandmothers do.
They say they will stay friends.

White Marine Corps vet Michael Woods gathered thousands of his brothers and sisters
to stand with the Water Protectors at Standing Rock.

Guns too heavy for my hands.
Can't imagine pulling the trigger.

What Matters

Newsfeed chock full of
hashtags about
Baltimore versus
draft riots
Red Summer
Black Wall Street
Rosewood
toy guns
who
what
matters
where.

What matters now
is me
running water
shea butter soap on skin
shea butter shampooed softness
hugging fingers,
head tilted back,
hair dribbling.

No comb.
No gel for hold.
No wraps for control.

As I head out for another day
to battle -isms
every z-shaped curl
will stand up and out

Let 'em
wonder
what walking
brown sugar
tastes like.

For the Record

My grandniece Carla is always reading.
Today she asked if I ever saw Billie Holiday perform.
"No, darling, I never did," I said. "Why do you ask?"
"The times we're living in," she said, "I need my heroes and she-roes."
She relayed an article about Lady Day and Harry J. Anslinger.

Didn't surprise me.
They promised us 40 acres and a mule and didn't give us anything
but a hard time and a short time to get there.

Never knew about Anslinger and his agents
setting Billie up for drug busts
because she wouldn't stop singing Strange Fruit,
that despite imprisonment
denial of her cabaret license because she might harm the public's
morals, being barred from the stage by many club owners,
she made Strange Fruit the last song of her set.

Waiters stopped serving.
Crowd stopped talking.
Total darkness.
Spotlight.
Had I known, I would have gone to Carnegie Hall to witness her
buttercream complexion
deep-set eyes
gardenia-graced hair
as she remembered her daddy,

the lung-damaging mustard gas he inhaled during the War
and him dying in Texas from pneumonia
because the hospital didn't treat blacks.

Never lowered her head in any photo I've ever seen.
Tilted her head back as she sang.
Carla said, "She couldn't read music, but knew,
to play an instrument well, posture matters."
Seen so many things change over my 99 years, except
that our people pay a heavy price.

Carla told me Billie knew they would kill her.
That last time in the hospital,
after they handcuffed her
took mugshots
confiscated her gifts of flowers, record player, magazines, and
chocolates Anslinger's men stopped the doctors from giving Billie
the methadone that was helping her get better.
She died days after.

"Auntie L," Carla said,
"Judy Garland publicly mourned Cynthia, Addie Mae, Carole, and
Denise, and requested funds for the families in '63.
If Judy knew how Anslinger persecuted Billie at the time
he asked MGM to give Judy time off
to recover from her heroin addiction,
might Judy have told Anslinger that Billie was also

a very fine lady who could have used some rest?
You think Judy might have sung him
a few bars of Strange Fruit herself?"

I said we'll never know
if Judy might have been moved,
or could move Anslinger.
Most likely he would have still boasted
about there being no more good morning heartache for Billie.

Maybe if our people knew what Anslinger put Billie through when
President Kennedy gave him a citation for outstanding service in '62,
there would have been a million brooms
bashing picture frames of JFK's face,
broom bristles scraping glass shards into dustpans,
our jaws set tight, murmuring
It had to be done.
We may have cried a little softer that next November.
Wish I had known
Billie called Louis McKay
a dirty motha-nevermind.
He hit her.
Sometimes they taped up her ribs afterward so
she could stand up straight,
tilt back her neck pretty and sing,
that when Billie got tired and cut him off
he called her a low-class bitch.
Said nobody was going to make a fool of him,
good as he'd been to Billie,

that if he got a whore, he got money from her or
he'd have nothing to do with the bitch.

I wouldn't have been
screaming
swooning
when Billy Dee stretched out his arm and fifty-dollar bill.
I'd have petitioned Berry Gordy to drop Louis McKay as
technical adviser for Lady Sings the Blues, redo that whole movie.
I'd have boycotted if he refused.

"We pay a heavy price in this country," I said.

Carla replied,
"Billie understood that music beguiles the memory in
ways authority never could."

They'll remember me.
When this is all gone,
and they've finished badgering me.

And we do.
Her trill,
willowy push
pull of every note,
every song,
the spotlight rendering her beacon,
a light in the dark.

Fixed

Not even rain was going to stop me
from staying all day at the greenhouse

amongst fluttering flashes of orange and yellow
on leaves, flowers, and nectar trays.

I read somewhere that butterflies
flap their wings faster than humans blink their eyes.

It is confirmed.

On Your Departure

Be blue lava. Be
Black opal. Be red beryl.
Be jadeite. Be.

Afterword

Nine years passed between the first edition of my first book, *Gnat Feathers and Butterfly Wings* in 2008, and the first edition of my second book *Thirty Dollars and a Bowl of Soup* in 2017. I wrote poems occasionally during those years, and had a few published, but I did not feel ready to publish another book.

Life happened. Motherhood and teaching demanded most of my time, and I spent three years earning my Master of Science in Adolescent Literacy Studies from Lehman College in 2016. After my graduation, I took stock of my life: a young adult son with a college degree, a solid career as an educator, two master's degrees, my health, and loving family and friends. God has abundantly blessed me. However, as I read through the journals I kept over the years, I was saddened by how often I felt unseen in thankless personal and professional relationships or by society-at-large as a Black woman.

I decided to write poems in praise of the things in life that are undervalued and compile them into another book. As always, my love and admiration for my family, friends, and students made their way into my poems, as well as my rage about the myriad forms of oppression. Dating was extremely interesting and challenging, and those experiences, good and bad, inspired numerous poems too.

The title, *Thirty Dollars and a Bowl of Soup*, came from a story a musician told me about America's underappreciation for its artists, and it is symbolic of this book's premise--give everyone and everything its due. I hope that future generations not only honor their independent artists but continue to dismantle the systems that diminish the quality of life.

Every one of you that has bought and read this book has honored me and my artistry, and I am forever grateful.

The Author

Carla M. Cherry is a native of the Bronx, NY. A graduate of Spelman College, New York University, and Lehman College, she has been teaching in the New York City public schools since 1996. Her poetry has appeared in various publications, including Anderbo, Eunoia Review, Dissident Voice, Random Sample Review, Firefly Magazine, Picaroon Poetry, Streetlight Press, MemoryHouse, Bop Dead City, Ariel Chart, Anti-Heroin Chic, The Racket, and Raising Mothers. All five of her books of poetry were published by ii-Publishing, which includes: *Gnat Feathers and Butterfly Wings*, *Thirty Dollars and a Bowl of Soup*, *Honeysuckle Me*, *These Pearls Are Real*, and *Stardust and Skin*. She is an M.F.A. candidate in Creative Writing at the City College of New York.

CONNECT WITH ME:

Email: carla.cherrybxpoet@gmail.com
Website: www.carlacherrybxpoet1.com
Facebook: @poeticchic
Twitter: @carla_bronxpoet
Instagram: @carlabxpoet1

Publication Credits

"Marks", "Hands", "Teal", "Thank You, Amber Rose", and "Objectified" were originally published in For Harriet.

The original version of "I Shouldn't Have Been There" first appeared in Obscura.

"Privilege" and "Cold Blooded" originally appeared in Eunoia Review.

"How Far We've Come" and "No Access" originally appeared in Dissident Voice.

"Diaspora" originally appeared in Random Sample Review.

"Love Letter" originally appeared in Bop Dead City.

"On the Mend" originally appeared in MemoryHouse.

"Common" originally appeared in Down in The Dirt magazine.

"Against the Grain", "Tamale", "Out of the Ordinary", "First Time", "Yankee Girl Reverie", and "Aftermath of the Great American Celebration" originally appeared in In Between Hangovers.

"Redress" originally appeared in Anti-Heroin Chic. "Bonanza" and originally appeared in Writer's Egg. "Diastema" originally appeared in Terra Preta Review.

"For the Record" originally appeared in Volume Four of The Bronx Memoir Project anthology.

www.ingramcontent.com/pod-product-compliance
Lightning Source LLC
Chambersburg PA
CBHW071822080526
44589CB00012B/883